GRUESOME EVIDENCE

According to many of his neighbors, Ray Copeland had worked around a lot of wells, repairing some, filling and capping others.

There was an old well near the Joe Adams barn and the investigators decided to re-check it. During the initial investigation, the water level had been high in the forty-feet deep well, but had gone down considerably since.

The deputies rigged a grappling hook and dropped it in the black water dozens of times before they finally snagged something other than trash or brush.

They pulled up a cowboy boot—with a foot still in it.

"Jesus," an officer quietly muttered as the boot and dismembered foot fell out on the frozen ground.

THE COPELAND KILLINGS

TOM MILLER

PINNACLE BOOKS
WINDSOR PUBLISHING CORP.

PINNACLE BOOKS

are published by

Windsor Publishing Corp.
475 Park Avenue South
New York, NY 10016

First Printing: January, 1993

Printed in the United States of America

Prologue

The system was slow, but effective.

Using a four-foot long thin steel rod, Deputies Kurt Reith and Paul Stegmaier poked the ground inside the old barn, creating a patchwork of quarter-inch-wide indentations as they worked their way from one end of the structure to the other.

The officers were searching for signs of hidden graves: hollow or sunken spots, too-loose soil, the clink of bones rotting under the barn's dirt floor. They followed the routine with little hope that they would be any more successful this day than the day before. For the past seven days, these deputies and scores of other deputies and Missouri State Highway Patrol officers had searched for bodies over a wide area of northwest Missouri's Livingston County. The search had yielded nothing other than a few old animal bones and the remains of at least one cow.

"You really s'pose anybody's in here?" Deputy Reith asked his partner. "I mean, if I was going to bury somebody, it'd be outside, somewhere where the sun shines, where a critter might carry off the evidence."

The unspoken fact this late evening of October 17, 1989, is that if the intensive search for bodies doesn't yield something—and real soon—the entire search operation would be called off, and the sheriff and his men were going to have a lot of red-faced explaining to do. It had been impossible to keep secret a several-mile-wide search for bodies, involving as many as forty officers. Backhoes digging in farm fields, surrounded by sheriff's cars and uniformed officers, was hard to keep quiet. While Sheriff Leland O'Dell had tried to be coy with the press and not really tell exactly what his officers and others had been searching for, it'd become common knowledge that bodies were the prey. No bodies meant big-time embarrassment, and the politically savvy Leland O'Dell knew that all too well.

So the search work continued.

The sunlight on this cold October day filtered through slightly open doors and cracks between the slats siding the steep-roofed white structure. A musty smell mixed with the sweet aroma of stored hay. Hand tools and coils of rope and wire were strewn against the interior walls, and heavy wooden beams lined up along the inner walls, holding the high roof. At one end of the hay barn was a small corral, built to care for or feed animals.

The barren ground—strewn in places with gradually rotting hay and straw—was hard-packed from years of traffic by people and livestock, run-down tractors and dusty combines. A long warm spell this late fall had suddenly ended, and harsh winter weather had set in, adding a dreariness to the terrain that comes back every year. The skiffs of ice on roadside ditches, with their patches of black and gray and white, provided about the only telltale color on the landscape this time of year. The corn and wheat fields were now no more than blown down stubble, and the reddish and white cattle that had not been sold or butchered clumped together near barns or bare tree groves.

The spacious barn, owned by farmer Neil Bryan, was a big, high-pitched roof hay barn, located some twelve meandering miles along county roads from Chilicothe, Missouri. The barn sat alone in a treeless field, on a farm just south of Highway 36 and nearest to the post office in Ludlow, Missouri. In a sense it stood as another rural memorial to a farmer's big dreams decades earlier, a man hoping to carve out a high and handsome living growing beef cattle.

Like most farmers in this hard scrabble country—where more topsoil is washed or blown away than stays around for pasture

7

grass or corn—the dreams had faded as gradually but as steadily as the barn's paint. The harsh reality of dirty, long days of backbreaking work and few dollars had taken its steady toll on many farmers in these parts. Empty barns and once-handsome, but now-abandoned, homes dotted the landscape, surrounded by fences grown through with bird-planted cedars and tall brush. Jonquils still burst forth each spring around homes that hadn't heard a human voice in years. The changes that the economists like to call "economic readjustments" had come hard here, splintering family trees and taking the substance from countless lives with it.

Countless farmers gave up in that region in the early 1980s' their dreams reduced to a Saturday auction sale, where 4-H made mud scrapers and old television sets sold quickly to the highest bidder. Auction sale bills ("Antiques, Appliances and Farm Equipment!") fought for space on crowded bulletin boards in small town cafes and grocery stores. The auctioneers (all proudly sporting "Colonel" in front of their names) and their helpers worked hard at not appearing to crow about their good luck at someone else's expense.

Those farmers who had survived, who stayed on the land, were either big enough or had stayed chummy with a banker or two so they could stay in the annual operating loan plans, or they were small enough that they had no risks and no huge bills and no one really coveted their little bit of a farm. Other survivors included those frugal few who refused to borrow against prosperity and inflated land prices in the 1970s, and they entered the widespread farm recession period with no debts hanging over them. Many of the survivors were older couples, the kids long gone to town or even big city jobs. They were left to survive by their wits, fighting arthritis to feed cows, keeping the old trucks and tractors running for another season, figuring out part-time jobs in town, hanging on to the only life they'd known. The Social Security check ended up being the first regular "paycheck" many of these farmers had ever received after decades of agricultural boom and bust.

Livingston County, Missouri, was as hard hit as any other by the farm depression. Angry farmers attended several noisy rallies there. Slowly circling their tractors and pickup trucks around the courthouse square, they listened to speakers urge emergency steps of some kind from the federal government, the lenders, and farm groups. Many found the bankers and the implied "conspiracies" of distant commodity traders to be a handy target of their anger and suspicions. When a banker was shot to death by an Iowa farmer at the height of the farm protests, more than a few farmers privately backed the embittered shooter. It was all frighteningly serious; even those who weren't farmers or in the farm supply business *finally* realized it.

There was also a hardness to many farmers in this part of the country, as if the land was winning in the age-old battle to farm it. Three counties west of Livingston, a group of farmers tied to the village of Skidmore gunned down a big-bellied town bully in 1981 as he sat in his pickup truck on the main street. The farmers and townsfolk stuck tightly together after the vigilante-style murder. To this day, no one has ever talked publicly about the crime; no arrest has ever been made. The coldness of the community toward outside snoopers is still fairly palatable.

Despite the hard times, the county and its remaining residents fought on, held together by church and home, by stubbornness and even bad luck. Many of the old farmers stay because it's all they know and it's where they want to be buried, their final surrender to the land. The country churches, with a small cemetery off to one side, still draw many of the longtime residents each week, the one stable part of their rapidly changing lives.

As in most rural northern Missouri counties, the residents cherished their privacy, their supposed insulation from the crime and mayhem of the big city. They could watch the murders and crime and upheaval on Kansas City television stations, but it seldom reached them. A standard line from residents of towns like Chillicothe is the pride in leaving doors unlocked, of not fearing drive-by shootings, of the freedom to drive the streets and visit the stores with little if any fear of violence.

That all changed . . . rapidly and tragically . . . in the fall of 1989.

Chapter One

This ordinary-looking, old, white barn on the Neil Bryan farm soon became the center of everyone's attention. Local residents would slow down for a long gaze at the structure, shaking their heads in disbelief, wondering aloud about what on earth had been going on right under their collective noses.

The deputies and their "punchers" were drawn to the barn as a bizarre investigation began to open in front of their eyes.

Six miles away from this barn, at the neat little yellow-sided frame home of Ray and Faye Copeland, police had asked the elderly couple some tough questions: Who were these men you hired to work for you? Where did they go? What's been happening here?

A gnarled, defiant, and generally sickly seventy-five-year-old, Ray Copeland maintained he didn't know anything about his temporary farmhands. His near-hysterical wife of fifty years, Faye, fretted nervously; one minute weepy, the next minute tough and hard, her cold eyes glaring back at deputies' questions in stoney silence.

The Copelands' forty acres of scrub brush, a couple of creeks, a small pond, and pasture land had been scoured. Baying bloodhounds had nosed around in sheds and fence rows and brush piles; as is usually the case with baying dogs in manhunts, this resulted in nothing. More than three dozen deputies and Missouri State Highway Patrol officers had poked around with shovels and staubs, followed by other officers with their heads bowed earthward to look for clues. A pair of noisy backhoes gouged out big sections of earth, but the only bones dug up were animal remains. Pickup trucks and sheriff's cars moved around the acreage, as officers clutched together in small groups across the farm. The county coroner, funeral home operator Scott Lindley, and the prosecuting attorney, Doug Roberts, were seen walking shoulder-to-shoulder with the uniformed deputies and patrol officers.

The Copelands had lived there for more than two decades, and two of their six children had moved back to the area in recent years. But little was really known about the Copeland family. Ray Copeland was usually gruff, crude, not given to glad-handed greetings in the cafes and grocery stores in nearby Chillicothe or elsewhere. There was seldom a smile seen on his deeply lined face, and it was rumored that he'd had some trouble with the law somewhere in his past. He was getting stooped as he got older, and often seemed to be hard of hearing, with a habit of cupping his massive left hand around his ear when he was talking to someone. He almost never wore a hearing aid, and he seldom treated other health ailments. He virtually always wore bib overalls. Faye Copeland had worked for a few years at a glove-making factory in Chillicothe and then cleaned rooms and worked the front desk in a discount motel. It appeared that the couple had few close friends; they seldom attended church or ate out together or were seen in social gatherings.

The Copelands, too, had money problems in the early 1980s, when small notes taken out by Ray came due and he didn't have the cash to pay the bank. He had made more than a dozen loans, apparently for cattle purchases, primarily at the First State Bank in Chillicothe. At one point, legal action was started against the couple, but they deeded their farm over to a son living in Arizona, and the financial crisis seemed to pass.

In this rural country, if you chose to be left alone, people didn't bother you. And, that seemed to be the choice the Copelands had made.

That privacy was rapidly coming to a sudden and disturbing end.

The search of the Copeland farm had drawn intense interest. Reporters were camped out at the end of farm lanes, and neighbors were keeping the telephone lines hot. Deputies already felt they'd uncovered part of the puzzle.

They felt sure that Ray Copeland had hired transients, the young rural men lost or adrift through small town America, to take part in a bad check scam at cattle sale barns. Ray Copeland didn't deny hiring help, and having a number of hired hands over the years. But officers now knew the men—maybe a dozen, maybe more—had opened post office boxes and local checking accounts. They had been seen with Copeland at cattle sales, had written bad checks to buy cows, and then had mysteriously disappeared.

Livingston County Deputy Gary Calvert had been quietly thinking through what he'd been investigating the past several months, and wondering to himself where it was going to finally end. Sheriff Leland O'Dell was increasingly nervous about blowing the big case and was often petrified of the TV cameras and probing questions from reporters. He just wanted the whole thing to finish . . . successfully and quickly.

Some of the "cafe cops" in Chillicothe and around the area had already branded O'Dell and his department as a modern day version of "Mayberry R.F.D.," and began taking perverse delight every day that nothing turned up against the Copelands. The TV reports kept detailing failed searches and no evidence, and many who heard those reports were delighted by that turn of events.

But a search warrant trip through the Copeland house had yielded a wide assortment of men's clothing, not all the same size, and none of it Ray's. Deputy Calvert, while usually keeping his thoughts to himself, had become convinced that Ray Copeland, perhaps with help from Faye, had gone well beyond simply being involved in writing bad checks with his farmhands.

Could it be that this old man, who looked like many a grandpa in this rural countryside, got rid of these unknown drifters? Could it be that the drifters didn't drift on, but instead where stopped short at this northwest Missouri farm?

Surely not here . . . not in a spot were siphoning gasoline and tavern fights were the big crimes of most weekends; not in a spot where sheriffs and deputies generally know who commits most crimes before the investigation even begins.

But the investigation into the bad checks

and the missing farm workers had taken on a life all its own.

A few weeks earlier, an aging drifter had called Nebraska law enforcement officials and said he'd been "run off" from the Copeland farm, where Ray Copeland had tried to kill him. He claimed Ray had aimed a .22 caliber rifle at him a couple of times, but never pulled the trigger. And, chillingly, he said that before he left the Copelands' employ he'd seen "a skull and a leg bone" partially buried on the Copeland property. He claimed to have knowledge that Mr. Copeland had killed as many as four farmhands; men hired, like him, from homeless shelters.

That call and subsequent conversations with the colorful and controversial caller allowed O'Dell and Prosecuting Attorney Doug Roberts to secure a search warrant to scour the farm acreage and the Copeland home. This was enough to arrest the Copelands on conspiracy to commit fraud charges and lodge them in the county's jail.

While officers searched fruitlessly outside on the Copeland acreage, deputies searching inside took out a 1950-vintage Marlin bolt-action .22 caliber rifle. Inside an empty Polaroid camera case, high up in a kitchen cabinet, officers found a small piece of paper in Faye

Copeland's crude handwriting. It listed the following men's names:

> Gary Misko — left
> the Big Fat Man — back
> Jim Harvey — X
> Jim Geer — back
> Wayne Freeman — X
> Jack Holiday — Back
> Robert Root — Back
> Thomas Park — X
> Paul Cowart — X

The names matched many of the names from the pile of mysterious bad checks Deputy Calvert had gathered over the past several months, and especially those followed by an "X."

After finding this list, the officers on the case knew they were on to something very big here.

During the investigation, police had received dozens of calls daily from neighbors, onetime employers, and longtime acquaintances of Ray Copeland.

Callers to the sheriff's office were describing places where Copeland had worked in a dozen-mile-wide area around his home near the tiny settlement of Mooresville. The spots were written down at the increasingly busy and cramped sheriff's office back in Chillicothe, as officers gathered more and more details. Many of the reports were ludicrous, trying to implicate others, even trying to find a link to an infamous serial killer, Robert Berdella, who'd been recently arrested in a sordid case in nearby Kansas City.

Inside a closed door back room of the Livingston County jail, a modern structure a block from the courthouse, the Northwest Missouri Major Case Squad, a unit comprised of a variety of lawmen called in on major crimes, pored over telephone leads. Prosecuting Attorney Roberts nervously watched the gathering of the data, at times getting in the middle of tracking leads or looking for patterns to develop.

One Copeland neighbor, Bonnie Thompson, called and claimed she'd watched the Copeland house with her binoculars for years, seeing "bums" and "winos" around the place for a while, and then not seeing them anymore. She was afraid the Copelands were hiring lawbreakers, people who might endanger the quiet and the morality of the community.

Inside the Bryan barn, the ground search droned on.

"Whoa, whoa!" Deputy Reith suddenly shouted. His steel rod had gone down a few inches into too-soft soil. "Something here."

He lifted the steel rod and stabbed back earthward several times. The soft ground was becoming outlined.

"Get the shovel."

A shovel is the one thing the deputies didn't have. Deputy Paul Stegmaier's farm home was nearby, and he hurriedly left for a shovel, convinced now they'd found something. They weren't sure what they'd stumbled across, but it needed to be checked further and quickly.

Reith stepped out into the bright sunlight, took a deep breath, and used the car radio to call for help.

"Sheriff, we may have something out here. You might wanta come out to the Neil Bryan barn. And, uh, bring some, uh, tools . . ."

It was late in the day, the early October nightfall was near.

Thirty minutes later, the sheriff and his deputies began to roll in, driving past the TV cameras with straight-ahead looks and no comments.

"Whatcha think?"

"Dunno . . . could be . . ."

The shovel sliced into the ground too easily, and dirt was quickly shoveled out, to a depth of several inches by the fourth spadeful.

"Good God . . . look at this," Reith said in

a businesslike tone. "It's a damn shoe."

A well-worn, white tennis shoe was quickly laid bare, then another; the shoveling continued upward to reveal blue jeans and more. The shovel parted black plastic wrapped around the corpse.

The pit, the grave, was about ten inches under the bare barn floor dirt.

Quickly, the pace grew deadly serious. With the gathering crowd of deputies, as still as the corpse, the digging continued.

Tattered clothing, decayed flesh draped across bones was seen as the digging progressed toward the head of the body.

Not a word was spoken. A morbid silence grew heavy in the strained light of the barn. The head was bared.

A neat, small hole was found through the back of the skull.

"Jesus," a deputy muttered, hunkering down to examine the remains.

"Well," Sheriff O'Dell finally said, exhaling loudly after his word. "Better get Scott Lindley, and, boys, until we can say something, watch those damn reporters down the road, and keep this off the radio for awhile."

After a pause, as most heads are still drawn down toward the decaying body, the sheriff got back in the game.

"Better keep looking, may be more in here . . . God only knows what's been happening

22

around here."

Before the coroner could arrive, and only about a foot away, another grave was found, another body unearthed. This body, too, had a single bullet hole in the skull, was still dressed and partially wrapped in black plastic.

There's no identification on either body, no clue other than clothing as to who the men were.

A third body was uncovered.

The three bodies, while in separate shallow graves, were buried head-to-toe in a straight line at nearly the center of the barn floor.

Because it was nearly dark, O'Dell decided to halt the search, to leave the bodies in their graves until first light the following day. Deputies Reith and Stegmaier were to spend the night guarding the barn.

Aggressive television reporters, however, telephoned Neil Bryan, and were told that bodies had been found. The word was spread; no turning back now.

A few miles away, at the home of Wayne Copeland, one of Ray and Faye Copeland's six children, the telephone rang.

Wayne, not knowing what to believe about what he'd heard about his own parents, was puzzled, angry, and gut-sick all at once.

He picked up the receiver. The sound was

one he'd heard several times in the last few days: a scratchy tape recording of the Randy Travis country music song, "Diggin' Up Bones."

Wayne muttered an obscenity and slammed the phone down.

Chapter Two

The myth and the colorful folklore of the Depression-era Arkansas Ozarks survives even today: bustling little crossroads settlements, cheerful and robust families, hellfire and brimstone church meetings, boys and girls running happily through the hills, jugs of moonshine, and big, hard-working men tending the farm fields.

Even some of the town names are quaint, colorful images of the good, simple life: Flippin and Yellville, Hasty and Fiftysix, Bear Creek Springs and Mount Judea.

The Ozarks that Ray Copeland was brought up in had a much harsher, crueler side, however: failed crops, no money, no jobs. It was, for many families like the Copelands, a stark, cheerless, rugged life.

Ray Copeland was a strapping, tall young hillbilly, growing up in the rugged Ozark hills near Harrison, Arkansas, in the early quarter of this century. He had huge ears, and a hook nose that could cast a shadow across half his face. He never worried a whit about his weight, staying bone skinny no matter what food he put into his nearly six-foot, five-inch frame. Ray Copeland could make quite a presence. A few yellowing snapshots remain from those days, showing Raymond as a gangly, young man.

There are no smiles, though, just deep, cold stares at the photographer.

Some who still recall those days remember Ray Copeland as a hard worker with a strong back, but also as a youngster who had little truck with school, finally dropping out for good at around the fourth grade.

And, he was also, early on, a conniver; a young man willing to use his back to work hard, but also cunning enough to look for any scheme that could earn him a few bucks.

The average yearly income around Harrison in those post-Depression days was in terms of hundreds of dollars, and many didn't even dream that high. The fields that could be cleared of trees and scrub brush were row-cropped, some farmers found pasture room in the flattened out valleys between the knobby mountains, and others hacked out a living cutting oak and hickory timber.

Ray's parents, Jess and Laney Copeland,

moved the young growing family frequently, looking for work or places they could farm for a piece of the meager take. In the decades before the Okies moved west in huge numbers, the poor families tending the soil moved in a much narrower circle, finding work and food where they could. They were unskilled workers at the beck and call of the farm boss and owner.

Ray Copeland was born in Oklahoma in 1914. His family moved to northern Arkansas shortly thereafter, and young Ray grew up hard-nosed and as spoiled as a kid could be in a family that had virtually nothing.

"Never quite understood it all, but mom and dad always let Raymond get away with things that none of the rest of us did," says his older sister, Nellie.

One of his first crude ventures into livestock stealing came before he was twenty, when Ray Copeland stole a pair of hogs and sold them.

He stole them from his own father.

Ray Copeland took the swine from a muddy pen on the family farm one day when his parents were gone, likely working on the host farm where they lived. He rousted the swine out of the holding pen, quickly loaded them in the family's farm wagon, and then sold them in nearby Eureka Springs, Arkansas.

And, later on, he stole and forged WPA checks from his brother John and neighbors, cashing the thirty-one dollar documents with a forged signature. Ray Copeland had figured out what day the rural mail carrier would come by with the government checks designed to help poor Americans weather the Depression. He would stake out the mailboxes, either at his own home or sometimes at the homes of others, and steal the checks before they could be delivered to the rightful owners. He'd forge the names on the backs of the checks at the bank in town and pocket the money. As came to be his style, the system was crude but sometimes effective.

"He could look you right in the eye and lie to you, even then," John Copeland recalled about his kid brother in an interview years later. "He seemed to be looking for an angle, you know, a way to shortcut things. And, sometimes, maybe a lot of the times, Mom and Dad would know about it and wouldn't do anything, nothing at all." John Copeland, like others who remember Ray Copeland as a youngster, profess not the slightest shock whatsoever at what eventually transpired.

After he dropped out of school, Ray

started learning how to get by on his wits in an area that beat down farmers quicker than they could beat the rocks out of the scant soil.

While Ray Copeland dabbled in stealing checks or livestock, it could never truly be said he was very good at what he did. In 1936, when Ray was twenty-two, he was arrested in Harrison, Arkansas, and charged with forging government checks and sentenced to six months on federal charges and six months on state charges.

The big, surly Ray Copeland would saunter in and out of courtrooms and sheriff's offices with a noticeable smirk, an "I'm-smarter-than-you-dumb-cops" attitude that belied his getting caught and being convicted time after time.

Even after that initial conviction, his family recalls, Ray Copeland's parents stuck by him. They even bought his story that he'd been framed and that he was going to beat the system.

In the spring of 1940, he stopped by a doctor's office in Harrison, and met a young fair-haired girl waiting to see the doctor. Faye Della Wilson was nineteen and had never dated or even really known a man who wasn't a relative. In the dirt-floor cabin near the tiny crossroads community of Red Star where she and her family lived, a stern father forbade dating, required regular church attendance, and worked the kids very hard on the farm. Faye, a pretty, shy, hill girl, was mightily impressed by the big-talking Ray Copeland.

Faye's parents, Rufus and Gladys Wilson, raised seven children near Harrison. Faye went to school through the eighth grade and then dropped out to help her family. By the time she was ten she was working for others, doing laundry, cleaning houses, or baby-sitting.

Ray Copeland convinced Faye Della he had money (a rare commodity in those days in Arkansas) and she quickly fell for him.

"She came from a family that was really poor," Ray and Faye's only daughter Betty said years later. "And Ray, he was always braggin' about how good he was at making money. He could make you believe it, if he wanted."

Ray and Faye were married in the fall of 1940 by a judge in Harrison, Arkansas. Within that first year Faye gave birth at the couple's home to their first child, Everett Roy. Two years later, in 1943, Billy Ray was born at the same home.

In 1944, Ray took his fledgling family to rural Fresno County, California, and Betty

Lou, the first girl, was born in 1945.

Scouting for work, Copeland moved his brood back to Arkansas in late 1945, and their third son, Alvia Lee, was born there in 1947.

The Copelands moved back to Fresno County in the spring of 1949, and Faye delivered the couple's fifth child, William Wayne. The California moves weren't panning out for Ray. In the fall of 1949, they were back in Arkansas.

Family members old enough to remember believe Ray fled California this last time because he had been caught stealing some horses from a man he worked for. He was either dodging arrest or had worked a deal with the horse owner to leave the state. Nobody seems to recall the actual facts.

But the Arkansas move didn't work either, and Ray was arrested in late 1949 and charged with cattle theft, a charge of grand larceny lodged in Boone County, Arkansas.

A pattern that would dog Ray Copeland for the next half century started that year in Arkansas: he liked to steal livestock. Once a cow or pig is slaughtered or even resold, it was very difficult to prove ownership decades ago. Ray took great advantage of the honor system between those buying and selling the animals, where deals are often secured by a handshake and a check. He saw the livestock buying and selling operations as an easy mark, and saw the cash he could get from stealing livestock as pure profit.

Once again, at age thirty-three, he was convicted and sentenced to a year in jail.

Ray Copeland's young family was destitute, moving in for a while with Ray's brother John Copeland. There were times the family literally didn't have a dime to their names, and had to rely on welfare and food handouts to stay alive. The boys still remember welfare workers, or social workers of some kind, coming in to the home to give them haircuts at the kitchen table. Faye sometimes worked, scraping for a dollar here and a dollar there, and managed to keep the family together while Ray sat in jail.

In 1950, Ray was out of prison again, and apparently thinking about a new start. He moved his young family to the tiny town of Rocky Comfort, Missouri, in the extreme southern part of the state. Like northern Arkansas, the Missouri Ozarks drew farmers with acres of cheap land, privacy, and the hope of success through family farming. But by early 1951, Ray Copeland was back in trouble.

His early Missouri troubles continued his pattern: abusing trusts, betraying those who befriended or hired him. Those were still times in rural America that if a man said he'd work for you, and he had a family, you trusted him. Ray Copeland would establish the trust, befriend his new boss, then end up stealing from him.

In February 1951, he was arrested for stealing a calf from another farmer who'd hired him, then taking the calf across state lines to Eureka Springs, Arkansas, where he sold it.

But this time, Ray caught a bit of a break. Faye remembers that the judge "sentenced" her husband to work for a while on the judge's farm, avoiding more jail time.

The Copelands moved again, this time to Illinois in 1953, settling near the community of Brighton, then to the Bloomington area and other spots through the central and western portions of the state.

They moved frequently, and often suddenly, with little warning or preparation. His children now suspect that it was often done to avoid the law. "Dad would come in and say, 'Pack up, we're leaving in the morning,' " son Al recalls of those days in Illinois. "We went to so many schools I can't even remember them."

During that period in Illinois, Ray was arrested at least three times and was sent to a state prison farm for writing bad checks and for forging a personal check.

In addition to the legal troubles, Ray's anger and coldness toward his family grew. He seldom had time for anyone but himself, his family recalls, and he was increasingly given to fits of rage and violence that spared no one.

He was physical with the boys, often beating them, his huge hulking frame terrifying the youngsters. He ignored birthdays, Christmas, and other holidays. He shunned any show of affection. Faye was treated in much the same manner, told to do what he wanted and nothing more. She now says he often took great delight in telling her how stupid she was, when she was the one who could read and write and kept the family records. She seldom sided with the boys in the disputes, possibly as much out of fear of Ray as anything else.

The scene seems almost comical, more than three decades later. It was 1955, and a tall, skinny Ray Copeland is shown posing out front of the white frame farm home that he and his family were living in as part of the deal of working for an Illinois farmer. He's got a stringer laden with fat catfish, jugged from the nearby river. Fishing lines are attached to floating jugs in the water, and stinky catfish bait is balled up on the treble hooks hanging in the murky, barely moving river water. The jugs are left for a few days, in hopes that the catfish would mosey onto the hooks. It was the perfect way to fish for a farmhand who seldom had the luxury of a day off: the jugs could be checked, and the fish hauled ashore after work was done in the evenings.

And, in the always poor Copeland household, the fishing was not recreational but was for the supper table.

Ray Copeland, in his familiar overalls even in 1955, posed for the camera with his youngest son, Sonny, who nervously sticks a finger in his mouth when the camera snaps. Ray Copeland has rolled up the overalls legs to his knees, fresh from retrieving the bobbing jugs, and is standing akimbo from the weight of the fish.

The snapshot looks for all the world like another pleasant day on the farm for the big, happy Copeland family.

Pictures can, in fact, lie.

The tension, the anger, the violence in the

Copeland household in those days were routine moods. Ray Copeland was constantly in trouble, yet tried to beat the system. He didn't take any guff from Faye, and certainly had no time for the kids.

Sons Wayne and Al both have painful memories of those days on the Illinois farms, when chores could never be performed to their father's expectations, and they suffered the consequences.

On one farm in McLean County, Illinois, Ray Copeland was required to see that a small dairy herd was milked each morning and evening. The boys were, of course, required to help. In the early fall, their father had bought Wayne and Al "school shoes," which were the only shoes the boys had.

He wouldn't let the boys wear the "school shoes" when they milked, despite the icy temperatures in rural northern Illinois winters.

"We went barefoot, even in the winter," Wayne remembers. "We used to mush our feet around in the cowshit just to keep them warm. He thought that was funny as hell."

Another time, when Al, eleven years old by then, was milking, the cow kept kicking her back leg shackles off, sending the metal devices flying and interrupting the milking routine.

"Dad come in and told me how dumb I

was for letting the old cow do that," Al remembers, "and then *wham!* He took the cow kickers and knocked me in the head with them. He did that kind of thing a lot, to all of us."

Al grimaces when he remembers breaking his wrist in a fall from a hay wagon while he and his father were gathering hay. Copeland made his son continue working through the day with the painfully swollen wrist, finally letting Faye take him to the doctor in the evening.

Faye spent every waking moment tending to the growing, hungry brood, and trying to figure out ways to earn money with part-time jobs.

She never crossed her husband, at least not that any of the children can remember. In fact, Faye wouldn't tell the children where their father was when he was in prison, telling them only he was "out of town" for awhile.

While the children suspect that maybe their mother occasionally argued with their father, they have no recollections of such moments.

"Mom just knew hard work, and she knew she was supposed to be loyal to her husband," Al remembers. "She did just that . . . out of fear of him, just like for all the rest of us."

But Faye Copeland was also the "brains" of the household, the only adult who could read and write. She was the record-keeper, the bill-payer, and some say, the one who urged Ray Copeland to provide more money to pay those bills.

The children wasted little time leaving home, and some have never looked back.

Wayne joined the Army shortly after Ray Copeland beat him with a hammer after a blow-up that involved farm chores. Daughter Betty married young, primarily to get out of the house and get away from her father. To this day, she can muster up support for her mother, but has nothing kind to say about her father.

In early 1961, Ray was arrested and pled guilty to writing a $2,960 bad check for twenty head of cattle he bought. He spent nine months in prison at Vandalia, Illinois.

In 1962, he repeated the offense, issuing a bad check for $1,934 for nineteen head of cattle in Ford County, Illinois. He spent another nine months in prison.

Ray had figured out that cattle auctions were largely based on an honor system, that it was surprisingly easy to write and cash checks for cattle purchases. He would seldom be asked to show identification; his personal check, or that on some other account, would be easily accepted; he would drive off with the cattle. He would then resell them to someone who'd give him honest money.

Given the nature of the cattle sales, in addition to the ease of writing checks, Ray could easily turn around and resell the cattle, usually the same day, and pocket the money.

He got caught continually because he was forging the bad checks himself. The "bad paper" could be traced to him, and he was spending more time in jail than out in the early 1960s.

He was going to have to change his system.

Chapter Three

From his earliest days, perhaps rooted in the envy felt by a poor Arkansas hillbilly, Ray had an intense hatred of banks and bankers. Many men of his generation had seen bankers sometimes bilk farmers and their families out of their land. In the days before encroaching and increasingly strict government regulations, bankers and, sometimes, lawyers became the target of anger and distrust from those trying to carve out a living from the ground. Most of those burned by the bankers during the Great Depression years, however, managed to get over their hatred and distrust of the bankers. They may have continued to sock money away in a lock box somewhere, but they came to accept the fact that the bankers they had known of in the 1920s and 1930s had changed. They were now perhaps a little more helpful and honest.

But Ray Copeland never changed his attitudes, however, and continued to be nearly obsessed by the games he thought he could play to "get" bankers and their ilk. Copeland came to believe that ripping off a bank, scamming a banker with a bad check or forged paperwork, wasn't really a crime. You couldn't, in his perverted logic, rip off someone who was already a tin horn crook. Bankers were fair game, period.

Ray had a habit of carrying around tattered newspaper and magazine clippings in the front pocket wallet that he kept in his bib overall pocket, next to his heart. Most of the articles concerned bankers and banks that had been bilked by insurance companies and scam-artists.

However, Ray was increasingly aggravated by the knowledge that he simply couldn't figure out a way to keep from getting caught. His enemy, those suit-wearing bankers, were still outsmarting him, with the help of the law, time after time.

He'd served five jail sentences in Illinois and Arkansas, and was finding the brand of criminal he was associating with to be younger, more violent, and uninterested in a tired old farmer who wrote bad checks and stole cows and pigs. In his younger days, a few months in jail weren't that distasteful. He'd have a chance to learn new tricks from other "paper hangers"; he'd have a chance to rest up and not have to rise with the sun and scrounge for a living; and he'd be away from his wife and children and their harping about needing shoes and groceries.

But, Faye Copeland was working too hard and says now she was getting increasingly sick of Ray's run-ins with the law. Still the ever-faithful wife and mother, she continued to pack up to move with him, took any kind of job she could find to make a few dollars, and kept the family in beans and jeans. As the children got older, she grew even more mum about the activities of her husband. And, they knew not to ask too many questions.

When he was home, Ray Copeland was nearly always in his dark blue bib overalls. He still liked to flash, or at least brag about, his big wad of money. From his early teens on, Ray consistently carried his money in a wallet in the chest pocket of his bib overalls. He seemed to take great delight in telling anyone who'd listen that he'd beat the system, that he had money or knew how to get it. He used banks sparingly over the years; he was sometimes turned down for checking accounts and other services like farm operating loans because of his record of forgery and passing bad checks. He told his children to save money they'd earn from part-time jobs, then he'd raid their savings accounts, never repaying the "borrowed" money. He also stashed money away from the family, but there's little, if any, evidence he ever spent lavishly.

It seems that the "game" itself may have been the thing with Ray Copeland. He apparently never aspired to own big Cadillacs or take cruises to the Bahamas. He was intent on trying to win in his battles of wit against the bankers and the system. His victories weren't to gain financial rewards, but rather to get one over on his lifelong foes.

He seldom, if ever, mentioned his jail time to those he knew or worked around. Some who lived near, or worked with, Ray Copeland over the years would often be surprised to later learn he'd ever done jail time.

In the summer of 1966, Copeland and his family struck out again, this time settling in northwest Missouri for the first time, likely drawn by one of the all-too-frequent downturns in land prices and the local farmer's needs for cheap farm help. Maybe, too, he was hoping to start afresh, to break away from snooping deputies, banks and sale barn owners. Maybe, however, he just thought he'd find another spot to ply his trade, such as it was. Ray Copeland was then forty-seven years old. Faye said years later that she thought, this time, he was ready to just settle down and enjoy his family and go to work and stay out of trouble.

The Copeland family moved into a farmer's house in exchange for working for him. It was not uncommon in those days for farmers to hire hands, pay them scarce little money, but provide them with a run-down home, pay the utilities, and generally try to see to the welfare of the family. Implicit with those hirings, too, was the understanding that the hired hand could work any other type of job or angle he wanted to as long as the farm chores were done first.

About a year later, the family moved to another house near Utica, Missouri, about five miles west of Chillicothe. The four oldest children had left home, and Ray and Faye began looking for a small farm of their own. They'd never owned property other than automobiles, and Ray Copeland was learning about the area and knew which pieces of property were for sale and where a small home might be purchased for his family to set up housekeeping.

They found such a farm in late 1967, a small run-down home fronting forty acres with water and a pond. They put down a five-hundred-dollar down payment and agreed to make $40 a month payments for the acreage and house near Mooresville, Missouri. Their first—and last—home cost six thousand dollars.

The farm was located about two miles from Mooresville, a trace of a town. Founded at the turn of the century, with about 200 residents and a bank, the town hadn't grown much since. Dirt streets led back to a scattering of small homes, house trailers, and a pair of churches. A Community Building gave testimony to efforts to revive the community, or at least its spirit, over the decades.

The Copeland home was a one-floor, yellow-sided, plain-looking structure. When Ray was home, the family usually kept the place looking fairly nice. The Copelands also usually maintained a large garden, and had been known to sell produce (tomatoes, squash, and pumpkins) from it over the years.

It would become the family home for the next twenty-two years. When Wayne and Al both settled back in the Chillicothe area, the grandchildren would visit, and the wives of both sons at least tried to establish "normal" communications with the Copelands, despite the hard, old feelings of their husbands toward their father. The sons, Wayne and Al, grudgingly made some degree of peace with the old man, finally growing to realize that he couldn't really do anything to them now that they were grown and living their own lives.

Faye Copeland made most of the house payments, while Ray continued to stash his money in fruit jars and other hiding places around the house and farm. She recalled years later that she seldom asked him about "his" money and still claims to have had no idea what he did with it. There's now evidence that he constructed small pipes, with screw-on caps, to hold some of his money, devices that were apparently buried or otherwise hidden on the acreage. He wasn't about to let the banks have any of his money. He worked odd jobs for a wide variety of farmers and landowners, farmed when he could, and continued to attend the area's cattle and pig sales.

In 1972, Faye says the house was paid for.

Faye Copeland knew little other than hard work from the time she was born. She was a meticulous record-keeper, jotting down due dates for notes and loans on scraps of paper, keeping the birth dates of all her children and grandchildren recorded on a wall calendar in the family kitchen, and trying to keep track of Ray's deals with cattle, which often netted

47

few receipts or records.

Not long after the family moved to northwest Missouri, Faye landed a piece work job at the Midwest Quality Gloves Corporation, putting together work gloves alongside dozens of other women on an assembly line in an old building that was hotter than a laundromat in the summer months and chilly and uncomfortable in the winter months. Factories such as the one that employed Faye were usually drawn to rural Missouri by a willing work force of women, who would work for low wages, scoff at the notion of a union, and would show up for work regularly. She worked there from 1966 to 1977, and then from 1978 to 1983. She was considered a punctual and loyal employee, according to company work records.

After staff changes and cutbacks at the plant, Faye found herself out of steady work in 1983. Not ready to retire, and perhaps still concerned about her husband's ever-fluctuating income, she then applied for a part-time position at the Holiday Motel in Chillicothe.

Faye Copeland cleaned the small motel rooms, occasionally ran the front desk, and did a variety of other jobs for motel owner-operator Neeta Patel. Mrs. Patel had Faye baby-sit her children from time to time, and she found Faye always willing to work extra hours for extra money. As Ray spent a fair amount of time out of town at cattle auctions, Faye would often stay at the motel, sometimes for as long as eight or nine days at a stretch.

Few people remember many smiles from Faye, but they do remember hard work and few, if any, problems from her.

Deep lines etched her face over the years, and she seldom if ever made any references to her husband. Her one concession to vanity was fairly regular trips to the beauty shop to have her gray hair permed.

Ray Copeland was thought to be a pretty good judge of livestock, and liked to deal in them. Yet, despite his sharp eyes for a good sale, there's little evidence he ever made huge sums of money. It's not unusual for farmers and retired town folk to simply attend these sales, almost as a social outing, day after day, week after week. It was a chance to socialize, hear the latest news, gossip about other farmers and their families, and to keep up with the changes in the local farm economy and to, of course, fuss about the weather and the politicians.

But Copeland usually avoided the gab sessions, however, usually opting to sit quietly in the bleachers and watch the sales, or wander through the holding areas, taking a closer look at the cattle waiting to be sold. He may have been trying to work out more effective ways to work his private scams. In the early 1970s, Ray seems to have changed his plans a little, finally coming close to the scheme that eventually brought him down and put him on death row.

In that era, according to those who attended the same sales, Ray would start showing up at the various cattle sales with hitchhikers and drifters. The pair would sit apart on the sale barn bleachers. Ray would signal to the hitchhiker his intentions to buy a group of cows or pigs, tipping his hat in most cases to signal staying in the rising bid.

The pair would then buy the cattle, using Ray's reflective judgment as to when to buy or bow out of a rapidly rising bid.

Then, in a stroke of real brazenness, Ray Copeland would have the hitchhiker sign "Ray Copeland" to the check for the purchase.

The check would, of course, bounce, and Ray Copeland would have by then resold the cattle for "good" money, stashing it safely away. When the bank would eventually notify him of the bounced check, Ray Copeland would plead innocence by claiming—rightly, in fact—that the signature on the check wasn't in his handwriting. The sale barn would then, in most cases, end up having to cover the check.

Not very sophisticated, granted, but it worked dozens of times for the shifty old Copeland.

The hitchhikers soon disappeared from around Chillicothe after a couple of rounds of check-writing ventures. The assumption is that they simply drifted on, fifty dollars or so richer. No one, however, really knows what happened to those men.

It appears at the time of these incidents, Ray was traveling to the Salvation Army center in Bloomington, Illinois, near his old address in that state, and was hiring the young men for the buying and check-writing scheme.

One Missouri State Highway Patrol officer, Jim Rhoades, spent a couple of years on the puzzling Copeland case but was never able to nail him. "Boy, we really wanted to get him bad, but we never could get the thing put together just right," Rhoades now recalls. "He was a wily old bird, and he caught a few breaks here and there."

Many law officers from that era are now

convinced in their own minds that Ray Copeland was killing transients then, but was hiding the bodies in such a way that they never would be found. He was also younger and more mobile in those days, and might have traveled much farther to find burial spots for his victims. Those days also predate more sophisticated banking and law enforcement procedures that link agencies and banks by computer and help in quickly tracing bad paper and establish links between crimes.

Trooper Rhoades did find one drifter involved in the check-writing scheme, a young man named Gerald Perkins. Perkins made a detailed statement to officers in early 1970, outlining what he said was Ray's scheme, and Rhoades thought maybe this time he'd snag old Ray Copeland.

Perkins told officers that Copeland had identified himself as a big-time cattle farmer from Missouri who wanted to teach young men "the cattle business." He was offering them three hundred dollars a week plus room and board, which was serious money for farmhand work.

In his rambling statement to officers, Perkins said Ray Copeland was using pre-printed checks with other names on them, and having Perkins forge the signature after the cattle or swine were purchased. Perkins, of course, was hardly an innocent bystander in the scheme, obviously aware that he was forging a signature, but Copeland had more than likely convinced him that some way or another the check would be made good.

Perkins told officers he went to livestock sales in Sedalia and Gallatin, Missouri, and signed checks Ray Copeland gave him with the signature "Ray Moore." Other names that have surfaced from that period include "Roy Rollins" and "Stanley Rostron," and the name "William Hull" was also found on a few bad checks.

In those days, Ray Copeland was apparently operating by stealing blank imprinted business checks, again from people who had employed him or trusted him, and using the transients to forge signatures on them.

Copeland was arrested at one point in 1970 after Perkins gave officers his statement, but the case was never prosecuted. Rhoades remembers, "We couldn't keep Perkins sober long enough to get the case to trial. It was real frustrating, but we kept a close eye on old Copeland after that."

In mid-1970 he was arrested on a check forgery charge, and again in 1971 another forged check led to his arrest.

It was the 1971 arrest that led Faye to one of the few times she says she spoke up to Ray, according to her recollection.

She bailed him out of jail in faraway Ozark County, near the Arkansas line, and says she told him "If you ever get in any trouble of any sort, I will not help you. I will not even be around for you, because I don't believe in getting in trouble."

It seems her warning may have been heard, at least for a few years. There is no record that Ray was in any more trouble through the rest of the 1970s. But most long time law enforcement officers feel to this day that he simply got away with his schemes in those years, able to ditch the bodies in more remote areas, able to cover his tracks a little more skillfully.

But, even if he was staying on the straight and narrow, by the mid-1980s things began to sour for him in a big way.

Now past seventy, Ray Copeland was diabetic, his back hurt, his hearing was fading fast, and loans he'd taken out against the farm were coming due. The loans were short-term affairs in the few thousand dollar range, with the money apparently to be used to buying and dealing in livestock. He tried using the legal system in his cattle buying, and it was coming asunder on him.

Ray Copeland faced bankruptcy, and a Chillicothe bank was seeking to recover twenty-five thousand dollars in delinquent loans. He was able to shift a little of the liability to his wife. But Faye and her sons convinced Ray Copeland to consult a lawyer as the financial troubles mounted and after the bank filed to recover their loans. The Copelands went to nearby Chillicothe and hired attorney Doug Roberts, who was also the prosecuting attorney who would later issue the murder and conspiracy warrants against them. They walked in his small office a block from the courthouse and sought his help. In most of Missouri's smaller, rural counties, the prosecuting attorney can also maintain a private practice on the side, usually needing the extra business to make a decent living. Most of the side work is usually confined to writing wills, drawing up sales contracts, and referral work for other specialized lawyers. Doug Roberts was working with the Copelands, trying to come up with an arrangement to repay the overdue debts through another lawyer in St. Joseph, who specialized in bankruptcy cases. Then the prosecutor left town to take a pre-scheduled vacation trip.

When Doug Roberts returned, he discovered

that the Copelands had transferred with the help of another lawyer the deed to their farm to Sonny Copeland, and the latest financial crisis appeared to have been headed off. A repayment schedule was apparently drawn up, and the Copelands were able to stay on the farm and keep their home.

But by the mid-1980s, Ray Copeland had hatched up his most sinister scheme yet, deciding to chuck the banks, the loans, and the lawyers.

He'd do it his way, just as he usually had. He'd make the banks—and his hired hands—pay instead.

Chapter Four

Al Copeland had a peculiar, painful, love-hate relationship with his father, much like the other five Copeland children. The big, overbearing figure of Ray Copeland demanded some kind of grudging respect, and even fear, especially from the young children. Al dutifully worked farm chores with his father, and occasionally attended livestock sales, farm auctions, or went shopping for farm supplies with him.

One day in Illinois, when Al was barely a teenager, the two were riding in the pickup truck, when his father spotted a hitchhiker looking for a lift along the shoulder of the farm-to-market road. The young man was obviously down on his luck, and appeared to be carrying all his earthly belongings in a small suitcase at his feet.

The hitchhiker didn't get a ride from Ray Copeland, but his ears would have been burning if he'd known what the crusty old Copeland said about him. "Welfare bums," Ray snorted. "All they do is live off the taxes and drink and bum around and sponge off'n everybody else."

Al, as usual, kept quiet, nodding tacit agreement. The truck droned on down the highway.

"They oughta be got rid of," Ray continued, picking up a head of steam in his dashboard preaching. "Ain't too sure it wouldn't be doing ever-body a favor to just take 'em out and shoot 'em, just shoot 'em down, just get rid of 'em."

Those chilling words come back time and again to Al Copeland as a mild-mannered, good-humored adult. As a grown man, he is still trying to figure out what continually drove his father to evil, why his father continued to think he could beat the system and outsmart the law, when in fact he kept getting caught.

In his own way, Ray Copeland was drawn in deeper toward what he finally conceived as the ultimate victims: men who had destroyed their roots and had no future.

"Transients" has become the politically correct word for these men — and the vast majority of the homeless in rural America are men—as they drift through the countryside. Low-skill farm jobs, usually paid in cash with no records kept, continue to draw men for short-term work, a few days of regular meals, and a place to sleep. In addition to the farm jobs, helping to plant or harvest crops, clean up or destroy old buildings, and cut brush or timber, the rural economy also means summer jobs traveling with small carnivals, playing steamy hot parking lots and small town fairs. The carnival jobs also usually pay cash hourly rates, no questions asked, and carnival operators seldom if ever want to see an employee's résumé. In addition, agencies that aid these homeless men and sometimes their families are not as overburdened in most of the rural areas as they are in the urban centers. This means there's usually free hot meals and beds in the small town centers, and the small town churches and their ambitious, tub-thumping preachers are good for a few dollars, a meal or two, or maybe an odd job for a few days.

Unlike the much more visible urban homeless, most of the rural homeless prefer their anonymity. Most of them would just as soon blend into the woodwork as be out front and found out. They were indeed the perfect mark, the perfect victims, for Ray Copeland's final scheme.

From a distance, the men would simply pass for country farm workers, young men in town for an errand or to take a break from a day's hard work.

Up close, however, the differences are often more noticeable: the shoes somehow don't look like they exactly fit. The pants may be worn, stray stitches holding a ripped pocket in place, the cuffs only partially tacked up, the design of the clothes perhaps from another time and place. The jacket may have the same questionable air about it, like it was once worn by a growing high school boy somewhere. A garish tattoo or ragged scar might occasionally appear on one of the men, marks usually absent from those who stayed close to home.

Acting for all the world like a drunk desperately wanting to convince the world he's sober, most of the rural drifters want to silently convince one and all they're just a step away from turning things around.

And, despite a life of bad break after bad break, they're convinced that a good break is just around the next homeless mission, that all that separates them from the guy on "Easy Street" is a little good luck. So when the opportunity presents itself to rip a little off from the guy on "Easy Street," they take it.

Most are young, still with the legs to continue to run and hide. Their eyes, however, are older than the rest of their bodies, betraying fears and paranoia about what's happened and what's likely ahead.

While it's far too easy to generalize about all the rural homeless, some patterns do exist. Most have had at least brushes, if not outright run-ins, with the law. Most have had a tough time keeping relationships going; most have trouble with booze or drugs or both. Most have little education and leave little or no paper trail. And, most are easily mobile and wanting to stay that way.

Because of the depths many have fallen into, they don't want to face family or the old haunts just yet. The pride's usually still there in the hope that one of these days things are going to turn around. The long-held dream of someday getting things back together and strutting back home in a long Cadillac keeps many on the road.

Ray Copeland had tried stealing cattle and selling them himself. He'd tried stealing payroll and government checks and forging the signature. He'd tried finding drifters and using them to forge checks to buy cattle, quickly reselling the critters and pocketing the cash.

61

None of those schemes worked for very long. Ray Copeland kept getting caught. He kept going to prison.

It was time now for the *ultimate* plan.

In the mid-1980s, it gradually came to him: He'd find drifters, those aimless young men who roam the countryside, the guys who'd be called homeless in the big cities; guys who'd work for a day or two for cash and then drink it away or travel on.

Ray would promise them cash and a place to eat and sleep, telling them he needed their help in his cattle buying operation, a speech similar to the ones he'd used successfully in the past.

But this time, he was going to stay clear of the banks and the bad checks, and he hatched the final touch to his latest scheme: He'd have the drifters open their own post office boxes for an address. Then, they'd open checking accounts in their own names, and he'd have them write the bad checks for the cattle.

Once that was done, and the scheme was run a few times, he would need to get rid of the check-writers themselves. Cattle, stray dogs, and wildlife were easily destroyed around most farms with a single shot to the back of the head from a small caliber, usually .22 rifle. Neat and simple.

In a run-down section of Springfield, Missouri, the Victory Mission was a refuge for the rural drifters. It was one of a series of refuges for the homeless and those down on their luck along Commercial Street in the northern part of this otherwise booming city of 150,000 in the commercial heart of the tourist-rich Ozark mountains.

The Victory Mission would serve as many as 165 people a day, and was fertile territory for Ray Copeland in his search for workers. Bars protect the front windows of the mission. A heavy religious atmosphere is around the place, with regularly scheduled prayer and hymn services. Those men wanting a free meal were required to sit through the services. "How Great Thou Art" could often be heard coming slightly off-key from inside the mission as the men literally sang for their supper.

Rooms could be rented or borrowed, and meals were available three times a day. The warm smell of food permeates the place, steam coming from tubs of chili or soup or huge pots of canned vegetables. Kevin Gleason ran the mission and asked few questions of those who showed up at all hours of the day and night.

The mission also doubled as a source for

information on how to get welfare or other benefits and served as a base to land temporary day-labor work. Lumber yards, small factories, moving companies, all were regular visitors, hiring men for a day or two of hard work and cash pay.

Dan Pease, who was chaplain at the mission in 1988 and 1989 when Ray Copeland was a regular and persistent visitor, remembers the elderly Mooresville farmer coming around.

"He'd work the dining tables, going from man to man, telling them he'd pay them fifty dollars a day to drive a cattle truck, or some routine like that," Pease recalls. "He was real tight-lipped when I tried to talk to him about what he was doing and to sort of check him out. He just grunted or nodded, nothing much more than that."

Pease, like many of those who devote their lives to helping others down on their luck, was protective of the men, hoping to help them get back on their feet. The occasional success stories keep the men like Dan Pease going. Like others, he wasn't sure Ray Copeland was a person who was going to really help his charges.

Copeland knew about these places, knew what he was looking for, knew the routine by now all too well. He had a knack of quickly gaining the men's trust, convincing them he was a person who could help them get their lives straightened out.

By the summer of 1989, Ray Copeland had become a regular visitor to the Springfield mission, and to similar missions and seedy areas of town in Missouri and Illinois.

His approach was simple, low-key, and appealing to many of the men and boys who drifted through the missions.

"I'm getting old, and am hard of hearing," he'd tell the prospects. "I need someone to help me buy cattle at the auctions, and I'll pay you fifty dollars a day plus room and board." No questions asked, no paper trail, no chance of being found.

He'd add a few conditions. "You have family? Can you stay at my place and avoid contacting anyone? I want you to work for me and to not tell anyone where you are. I don't want a bunch of your kinfolk traipsing through my place, y'know?"

Again, for many of the men hanging out at the mission, those were conditions they actually preferred. Few of the men were eager for families and others to know where they were these days, and Ray Copeland's plan filled the bill: cash money, a little work, no string attached.

Driving his 1984 pickup truck, and dressed

in his usual blue Big Mac bib overalls, the hulking Copeland would usually find some excuse to display a big wad of bills while talking to the men, usually managing to interject that he was a "big farmer, a big operator" who would treat them right. Faye was often with him, the men now recall.

It was not a hard sell. Many of the larger landowners in the rural Midwest actually follow a Copeland-like pattern of understatement, preferring overalls to fancy suits, an old truck to a Lincoln Continental. It was not unusual for the wealthiest farmer in many a small Midwest town to drive the worst truck and to do all his business in cash. The young drifters weren't taken aback by the Copeland routine at all.

Dennis Murphy grew up in Illinois, not far from the farming area where the Copeland family lived in the 1950s. He graduated from high school and even attended a little college for a while. He had trouble, though, staying in one place very long. He had worked farm jobs, was once a janitor in a hospital in Bloomington, and was generally liked by the people he met and worked with.

But, he was also given to bouts of troubles, drinking too much, missing work, fighting and arguing at both work and in the little beer taverns that dot this part of the countryside.

Murphy, at twenty-seven, had seen a once-happy marriage dissolve, and had seen scores of jobs come and go. By the summer of 1986 he was living with his grandmother, who was seriously working with the young man hoping to help him straighten things out. He was living there when he was initially contacted by Ray Copeland.

Ray Copeland offered him big money, all in cash, to help him buy cattle. Dennis Murphy climbed into the pickup and headed to Missouri. His grandmother protested loudly, but to no avail. She knew rightly that away from her stern guidance, Dennis Murphy was taking a chance of seeing things fall apart again.

But Murphy ignored her pleas. The day Ray Copeland and Dennis Murphy got back to the Chillicothe area, Copeland took Murphy to the tiny village of Ludlow, population 147. County Route D is the main drag of the little farm community, only about nine or ten miles south of the Copeland home place. The small post office is the newest structure in town, and is located only a few feet from the branch of the Chillicothe-based Citizens Bank and Trust, a small banking facility geared primarily to the area farmers and those who commute to work in Chillicothe. A block of long-abandoned empty buildings faces the bank, and the town's only store (the Ludlow Market) is across the street and a little north of the bank.

Copeland parked near the market, and gave Murphy his instructions: First go to the post office and open a post office box in your name, and then go to the bank and open a checking account, again in your name, with the post office box address.

He gave Murphy cash, pulling the money from a roll of bills in the flap pocket of his familiar bib overalls.

Dennis Murphy, a thin, dark-haired young man who "looked farm" and was dressed in the standard blue jeans and shirt that everyone else wore, followed his instructions. He could be a charmer when he wanted to be, and succeeded in his efforts first at the post office and then at the bank.

Opening the post office box was easy, and opening the checking account was not much harder. Dennis Murphy bounded out of the bank, paperwork in hand, a new address, new job and a bank account with money in it: He felt that things were starting to look up for him.

Ray had Dennis sign a blank check, likely on the pretense that Faye could clean out the banking account "if we should both die in a wreck or something." It was an appeal he successfully used with other transients he hired, and Dennis Murphy obliged.

The plan was now set: In the period before the preprinted checks arrived, Ray Copeland and Dennis Murphy "practiced" at cattle sales in the region.

At virtually every crossroad town across the northern part of the state is a small auction barn for the sale of cattle and pigs. The layout is similar: Divided wooden slat or steel bar pens and loading chutes for moving the cattle are outside; inside is a pit with an outside door. Cattle are led in by the drovers, who shout and prod the next lot of cattle into the dirt floor pit. Bleacher seats surround the pit, and off to the side or in an adjoining room is the cashier. Nearby is usually a small cafe of some type and bulletin boards advertising future cattle or swine sales in a wide area. In the winter, row-crop duties put aside, many farmers spend several days a week traveling to the cattle sales.

The sales are held on a regular schedule, and don't compete with each other so that buyers and sellers can make a regular sale route through the week.

Most of the barns operated on an honor system, with few questions asked about checks or identification, at least at the time Ray Copeland and his partners were working the sales.

On October 8, 1986, Murphy and Copeland went to work, traveling to the Tina (pronounced, in all too typical Missouri style, as "TIE-nah").

Copeland dropped Murphy off walking distance from the Tina Livestock Auction, so the two men would not be seen together. He said this was because people didn't like him, and would overbid him just to spite him. So, Murphy would be acting as Copeland's "agent" and buying cattle for him. Ray Copeland would signal Murphy when to bid with a tip of his hat or with predetermined hand signals.

At Tina that day Dennis, acting under the direction of Ray, bought thirteen head of cattle, writing a check on his new account for $2,784. Murphy undoubtedly knew there wasn't that kind of money in his checking account, but was likely assured by Copeland that a deposit would be made to cover the document. Ray Copeland then turned around that same day, and resold the cattle, pocketing the cash.

A week later, the pair traveled to other sales, buying a dozen cattle for $4,116 at the first sale, and then paying $6,832 for a group of twenty-three cattle at the second site. In both cases, Ray Copeland sold the cattle later that same day, or held them for a few days at his Mooresville farm, then pocketed the resale money.

By the time of the second week's work, the first check had already bounced, and the scheme was starting to close in.

Ray Copeland fixed that.

As Murphy worked in a field on Neil Bryan's farm October 15, 1986, Copeland took careful aim with his 1950-vintage Marlin .22 caliber lever-action rifle, and sent a slug through the back of the young man's skull. Murphy was wearing work clothes, his pants held in place with a cowboy-style belt buckle with the name "Dennis" engraved on it.

After making sure Dennis Murphy was dead, Ray Copeland wrapped the boy in black plastic sheeting from a roll he kept in the back of his old pickup. He removed all identification and jewelry (except for the belt buckle).

Copeland then retrieved a piece of rusty log chain about eight feet long, and an old concrete block with three holes through it, all stored that day in his pickup truck bed. He ran the chain through the block, and wrapped the chain three times around Dennis Murphy's waist.

After that grisly chore was done, Copeland kicked Murphy's body off into the forty-foot well that was near the work site where Murphy had died.

The well was capped with a concrete slab, with an eighteen-inch square opening. It was brick-lined, about three-feet at the top and coning out to about four-feet wide at its forty-foot deep base. Dennis Murphy's crypt was well-sealed.

The Dennis Murphy bad checks were the first ones to hit Gary Calvert's desk at the Livingston County sheriff's office, the first ones to raise the suspicions that something was going wrong here.

And, Deputy Calvert shouldn't have necessarily known of the bad checks, because they were written in neighboring Carroll County. But, when Carroll County authorities investigated the bad checks taken by the livestock auction, witnesses said they thought the unknown check-writer, this Dennis Murphy, may have been with Mooresville's Ray Copeland. Besides, the checks were drawn on a Livingston County bank, the one in Ludlow.

So Deputy Calvert paid his first visit of what would end up being many visits to the Ray Copeland farm out by Mooresville.

Calvert, in his usual low-key and unassuming style, went to Ray Copeland's door, and asked the old farmer if he'd ever heard of a Dennis Murphy.

"Sure have," old Ray said, somewhat surprisingly to Calvert.

Copeland said Dennis Murphy had worked for him briefly, and Calvert said he had documents showing that Murphy had written a series of bad checks at cattle sale barns.

Ray Copeland's reaction to those facts again surprised Gary Calvert.

"Fact is, I got a bad check on him, too," Copeland said, fishing up the check he'd had Dennis Murphy sign weeks earlier. "He wrote me a bad check, too. Sure hope you find him."

So do I, Gary Calvert said to himself.

Chapter Five

Ray Copeland likely felt completely confident that Dennis Murphy's body would never be found. There would be no reason for anyone to ever be around the isolated old farm field water well, and he felt certain that Dennis Murphy could be gone for months and even years without anyone seriously missing him.

So, the cattle money in his pocket, and Dennis Murphy safely and finally out of the way, it was time to continue with the evil scheme.

Bright and early the next morning, the morning after Dennis Murphy's body had been coldly shoved down the well, Ray and Faye Copeland drove back to Illinois, in search of another cattle buyer.

It didn't take long for the Copelands, again in Bloomington, Illinois, to find Wayne Robert Warner, at the appropriately named Home Sweet Home Mission in Bloomington.

75

The sometimes good-natured and personable Warner was older, a well-worn, much-traveled forty years old, and had a history of severe and frequent drinking problems. He had violent mood swings during drinking bouts, sometimes recalling his sordid Army time, including wartime duty in Vietnam. His frequent troubles had kept him out of touch with his family for years. But, because he'd grown up in rural Illinois, he knew about farm work, and probably understood what Ray Copeland wanted done. Those were two key factors for Copeland, and he quickly struck a deal with Warner.

Wayne Robert Warner sensed an opportunity after hearing Copeland's pitch. He sensed that this deal, *this time,* might be his way to finally find the good life, to break the pattern of drink and sobriety, to halt the self-destructive behavior patterns that had become almost routine. For most of the men Copeland talked to, fifty dollars a day, plus room and board, was like a dream come true, and Warner was no exception.

Wayne Warner had been seeing Laurie Ann Prather, 26, after the pair had met at an Alcoholics Anonymous meeting. The man was "honestly trying to get his life back together," she now recalls. "He was really trying to get things right, and he saw this deal with this Copeland guy as the chance he'd been waiting for. It's all so sad now, just how close he may have been to getting back on top of things."

Laurie Ann Prather and Wayne Warner planned to be married at Christmas time 1986, but Warner left with the Copelands in early November for his new job in Missouri. The wedding plans were put on hold. Warner was upbeat about his chances for success, and felt this might be the would-be couple's chance at making it. The marriage, their lives together, would be even better after this deal worked out.

Maybe setting up a new life on a rural farm in Missouri would remove them from the temptations of trouble so they could settle down and enjoy their lives, Warner reasoned. Laurie Ann shared his hopes and agreed to the brief separation.

After a few days in Missouri, Warner came back to Illinois, enthusiastic and positive. It could be, he'd said, he'd caught that gravy train they'd been looking for.

Then Ray Copeland showed up again to get him, saying it was time to get to work. The simple fact that Copeland came back, like he said he would, gave the couple renewed hope that this was the deal they'd been waiting for.

Warner told his fiancée that soon . . . in just a few weeks . . . he'd be sending for her and they'd set up their new home in Missouri.

But Ray Copeland, of course, had other ideas. The time when Wayne was back in Illinois was merely to give the printed checks from the bank a chance to arrive at Warner's new post office box address.

Once back in Missouri a second time, Copeland and Warner started the same cattle buying routine, spending slightly more than six thousand dollars at cattle sales at different sale barns. Because Wayne Warner was a little older, and had spent more time around farms and farmers, he succeeded easily in passing the checks, convincing the sellers he was an experienced farmhand who knew the ins and outs of the cattle business.

But by mid-November, the checks started to bounce back to the sale barns. On November 19, 1989, Ray Copeland drove Wayne Warner to the Joe Adams's barn, on the pretense of needing some help with chores in the old hay barn there. Copeland and Warner went inside the barn, and while Warner was doing whatever Copeland had asked him to, the old farmer leveled the same old .22 rifle at the back of Warner's head. A single slug smashed into his head, piercing his brain, killing him quickly and quietly.

Changing his disposal method slightly, he wrapped Wayne Robert Warner's body, still wearing a heavy winter coat, in black plastic he had loaded earlier into his pickup truck, and shoved the body under the wooden planks in one end of the barn, in an area where baled hay would soon be stored. Some hay bales had to be moved to place the body in its final resting spot.

The barn was later filled, as Ray Copeland knew it would be, to the rafters with two thousand bales of hay and straw. The body was well-hidden for several months.

Part of the reason many officers later felt convinced that Faye Copeland had a direct role in the killings surfaced with the Warner death. It's likely that Ray Copeland would have wanted someone in his truck, or outside the barn, to serve as a lookout. The work involved in shooting the men, wrapping their bodies, and then hiding and disposing of them took time. Many officers feel certain that Faye Copeland would have been the only person Ray Copeland would have trusted . . . or could have convinced . . . to be a lookout.

There's an unexplained gap in the Copeland

routine after Wayne Warner's death.

Investigators theorize that Ray Copeland either got a little nervous about the back-to-back shootings, or, more likely, that victims during that period have never been found. There were indeed some checks written during those several months, and the check-writers had never turned up. Officers didn't know if they had simply left town, and were still on the road, or if Ray Copeland had hidden their bodies so well they would never be found.

But, whatever happened in the interim, the routine started again, in the fall of 1988, this time in Springfield, Missouri, at the Victory Mission.

Jimmie Dale Harvey, twenty-seven, was in many ways a walking victim. Suffering from epilepsy, and the results of a motorcycle injury to his head years earlier, Harvey was from Springfield, but still hung out at the mission, despite the attention and concern of his caring and worried mother, Ann Netherton.

Jimmie Dale Harvey had trouble keeping jobs for more than a few days sometimes, and was often at loose ends. He even spent a year in jail on a burglary charge a few years earlier. He had finished a truck driving school shortly before Ray Copeland found him, but had not been able to land a driving job. He was just a young man who had never been able to get his life in any kind of order.

In short, he was another good victim for the old Mooresville farmer.

Ray Copeland promised him the same as he had the other men: Fifty dollars a day, room and board, and the chance to learn the cattle business.

He also asked, as he usually did, that Harvey not contact his family, that he not use the Copelands' address or phone number, and that he not drink or smoke in the Copeland house, conditions Harvey willingly accepted.

The same routine followed: A post office box address was established, and a checking account was opened.

Ray and Jimmie Dale started attending livestock sales, and Harvey passed nearly twelve hundred dollars in bad checks.

The end for Jimmy Dale Harvey came on October 25, 1988. Ray Copeland asked Harvey to help with some chores at the Neil Bryan barn, and Harvey willingly came along.

Once inside the barn, Jimmie had unwittingly turned his back on Ray Copeland, and within seconds a .22 caliber slug pierced his brain.

Ray Copeland had run out of places for bodies, and must have decided to go the more conventional burial route this time. He first wrapped the body in black plastic. Then, using a shovel he had in the bed of his truck, he dug a shallow pit near the center of the open area in the center of the barn, and put the plastic wrapped body of Jimmie Dale Harvey to rest.

It was time again to find another farmhand.

A week or so later, the same pattern was followed at the Springfield, Missouri mission. John Wayne Freeman, twenty-seven, from Tulsa, Oklahoma, crawled into Ray Copeland's pickup truck and willingly headed for the Mooresville farm and a better life.

Freeman's father had died in Vietnam, and the family had been disjointed ever since. Gullible, and constantly fighting alcohol problems, Freeman ended up at the mission midway between Oklahoma and Indiana.

Freeman had a fairly substantial work record, one always marred, however, by a sudden and unplanned departure. It was not unusual for him to blow up at a boss, or start missing work, or to go on a drunk he couldn't stop. He was fond of playing pool, and since beer and whiskey are usually sold in pool halls, he'd get into trouble. He had worked as a machinist in Tulsa, in a plastics plant in Indiana. He had made frequent trips between Oklahoma and Indiana, and would often run out of money or sobriety along the road and end up in places like the Victory Mission. He had an eight-year-old son whom he was traveling to see when he stopped that fateful last time in Springfield.

Ray Copeland, his confidence apparent, used the same pitch and the same routine on Freeman, and it worked. Freeman came to the Copeland farm, stashing his clothes in a closet crowded with the clothing of other workers no longer in the employ of the elderly couple.

The post office box and checking account routine was followed again, and Copeland and Freeman began attending the cattle sales.

Freeman passed about fourteen hundred dollars in bad checks for Ray Copeland, and then the checks started to bounce. On Dec. 8, 1988, on the pretense of working chores with Ray Copeland, Freeman was shot once through the back of the head and was buried next to Jimmie Dale Harvey in the Bryan barn.

The isolation of the barns, like that one on the Neil Bryan farm, played right into Ray

Copeland's plans. He could have fired a cannon inside the barn, and no one would have heard. And no one paid any attention to a pickup truck parked nearby or what appeared to be workmen coming and going from a farm field. And, if he had a lookout, as many officers believe he did, he could have continued his evil work uninterrupted.

In early spring 1989, Ray Copeland started the deadly cycle over again. This time he hired a young Arkansas man he found at the same mission in Springfield.

Paul Jason Cowart, a twenty year old who was originally from Dardanelle, Arkansas, had been eager to hear Ray Copeland's pitch. Cowart had dropped out of the Havana, Arkansas high school at the end of the eleventh grade and began the wandering that would fill the rest of his short life. He went on solo hitchhiking trips through Arkansas, Missouri, Oklahoma, and Texas. He eventually married, and he and his new wife moved to Oklahoma and Texas. Then the often-rocky marriage ended. "P.J." briefly lived in Monett, Missouri, and tried to get back with his wife, but once again that failed. He traveled to New York, and then back into the Midwest, working odd jobs and maintaining occasional and warm contact with his mother, Edith Chilen. He had been hoping for a break, a chance to get his life going once and for all.

"P.J.," as he was known by his mother and his friends, occasionally sported a small mustache, but still looked younger than his twenty years. His mother was a truck driver, and P.J. wanted to follow the same occupation, but had been unable to settle down long enough to get started.

"P.J." Cowart came by his drifting naturally. His father abandoned him and his mother when "P.J." was two years old, and Mrs. Chilen says his great grandparents were Gypsies who drifted across central Europe. "He always wondered what was over the next hill," she recalled years later. "He was a seeker, a traveler."

When Paul Jason would come through Arkansas, his mother would baby him, repairing his tattered wardrobe, buying him new clothes or shoes if he needed them, trying to get him to settle down and find a job close to home. His mother would often label the insides of his clothes, just like a mother sending a ten year old off to summer camp. She'd put the initials P.J.C. inside a couple of new shirts he bought around Thanksgiving 1988, the last time Mrs. Chilen had seen her son.

He called his mother from Springfield after he had been hired by Copeland and proudly announced his new job, his new chance to get his life right. "He said he would be making $400 a week," his mother remembers from that last phone call.

His stepfather, Gail Chilen, said he had often warned Paul about the dangers of life as a wanderer. And, he said, Paul expressed sadness to him, sadness that perhaps was a fateful glimpse into the future.

"He was all blue, when he was about nineteen, and said to me [one] day 'I have a feeling I won't live to 21,'" his stepfather recalls. "I told him, 'Now, don't you worry, you'll live as long as you're supposed to.'"

The first evidence authorities found of Cowart being hired by Copeland came in 1989, when he opened a checking account in his name at an area bank. The opening balance was, of course, money supplied by Copeland.

Printed checks were ordered, and Copeland and his new hired hand set out to look over cattle auctions, to learn the system that Ray Copeland said would benefit them both in the long run.

Before the banks, or Deputy Gary Calvert, could trace the checks back to Cowart or Ray Copeland, the young Arkansas man was executed, and became the third in the line of burial sites in the Bryan barn. As usual, it was a single .22 shot to the back of his head that ended Paul Jason Cowart's life.

What was not usual is that it appears Cowart may have been shot while sleeping in the Copeland spare bedroom, only a few feet from the bedroom used by Faye and Ray. When found in the barn grave, he was wearing only a shirt and his underwear.

To this day, there are still a few people, including at least two of her sons and her only daughter, who think Faye Copeland was only an innocent victim in the whole Copeland ordeal; she did only what Ray Copeland told her to do, and she was not involved in the brutal killings.

In court, defense lawyers argued that "Ray's business was Ray's business," and that hard-working, soft-spoken Faye Copeland had been shut out from his brutal doings.

However, law officers close to the case note several factors through this brutal several month period when Ray Copeland was executing his hired hands.

First, one of the victims, Paul Jason Cowart, was apparently shot and killed inside the Copeland house while he slept, in a bedroom about ten feet from the bedroom used by Ray and Faye. Cowart may have drawn his last breath within earshot of Faye Copeland's bed. It would be hard to imagine, the officers contend, the shots and the subsequent removal of the body being done without her knowledge.

Secondly, the infamous list found hidden in the kitchen, written in Faye Copeland's handwriting, has a fateful "X" by the names of those men who officers can prove died. Other names on the list have the word "back" after the names, indicating, at least to the investigators, that the men were taken back to the missions where they were hired or for some other reason left the farm alive.

And, Faye Copeland was with her husband of nearly fifty years on several of his trips to homeless missions in southern Missouri and central Illinois. According to the handful of workers who survived the sinister plottings, Faye Copeland was deeply involved in the setup for the workers: the checking accounts and post office boxes. And, she saw to the men's needs at the home, taking care of their clothing, preparing meals, checking on sales results when the men returned from the livestock markets.

Finally, investigators feel, Faye would have been the logical lookout for her husband while he went about his chores of executing and then burying or otherwise disposing of the victims' bodies.

Ray Copeland's plan to stay clear of the bad checks, of pocketing the cash from the "real" cattle sales, was working well for him.

But it had been far from perfect: There were at least a couple of men Ray Copeland should have avoided hiring.

Jimmy Page was working for the Copelands when the case finally broke open in October of 1989, and was likely only a few hours from having a .22 caliber bullet through the back of his head. He was able to fill officers in on the setup of the address and checking accounts before he hightailed it out of Livingston County and back to the relative safety of the Springfield homeless mission.

Another man who got away proved that Ray Copeland was getting desperate in his hiring methods. Ray Copeland's greed got the best of him when he hired Jack McCormick.

Chapter Six

Maybe it was inevitable that Ray Copeland and Jack McCormick would hook up somewhere along the line: Both were aging con men, both had a dark side, both were always on the prowl for any of life's shortcuts.

If Ray Copeland's weakness was money and violence, Jack McCormick's was whiskey. And, where Ray Copeland had a brutal, bloody side, Jack McCormick had a clownish side and a ready smile. When he wore a chin beard, as he frequently did, he bore a striking resemblance to a leprechaun.

McCormick had drifted from a once-stable family in Idaho after the death of his wife in the late 1970s, and had spent the ensuing years drowning himself in booze. He had worked in Alaska and Florida, he had sold his blood to buy wine, he had stolen cars and trucks, and then had been unable to recall where he had been.

But McCormick was still brighter than

most of the winos and rummies who frequented places like the Victory Mission in Springfield, Missouri. When he was off the whiskey and wine, Jack McCormick would be the only man at the plasma center who would sell his blood for twenty-five dollars and then could give a detailed explanation of the processes used to reuse the fluids.

He was, in the best country vernacular, a big fish in a small pond.

He had a gift of gab, a winning smile and a repertoire of slick lines as long as most arms. He could talk intelligently, or at least fake it well enough, about a multitude of subjects, from the daily news to fishing in Alaska offshore waters. He would be absolutely flat broke and still reach for a *Wall Street Journal*.

He had seen his fortunes yo-yo over the years of running and whiskey, from times when he'd have money and be clearheaded to times when he was totally blacked out.

In Alaska, he'd worked for good wages, but discovered they sold wine and whiskey way up North, too. In North Dakota, he'd worked for a funeral home for a while, only to be fired when he drove a casket and its occupant to the wrong cemetery and sat there while grieving relatives of the deceased were gathered at another burying yard.

He had worked for traveling small town carnivals at the depths of his luck, and had managed to help run homeless missions and church groups when he was on the upswing.

At a well-traveled fifty-seven, he had hopes of things settling down and somehow getting better. He had also developed superior street smarts and knew a good con when he saw one.

Inside the drab entry lobby of the Victory Mission, a studious-looking man sat behind the counter. Bald, occasionally with glasses, usually with a smile, sometimes with a neatly trimmed beard, sometimes clean shaven, Jack McCormick more or less ran things, at least to hear him tell it.

Older than most in the mission, McCormick stood out for other reasons: When he was "on" he was smarter than most of the men who hung out at the mission, much more outgoing and intensely serious about keeping his life together.

He was "on" the first time he met Ray Copeland at the Mission.

Ray Copeland, on one of his many trips to Springfield to hire young drifters, met Jack McCormick and was seemingly drawn to the outgoing man, despite McCormick's age and obvious history of drinking too much.

Jack McCormick conned the con man, and

before too many visits, Ray Copeland was talking to Jack McCormick about coming to work for him.

Jack McCormick resisted Ray Copeland's overtures for a few weeks and months, perhaps concerned that if he left the structured safe haven of the mission he might fall back into his old ways.

"He tells me he wants me to drive his pickup for him, to work cattle sales with him," McCormick recalls. "He said it'd be fifty dollars a day plus room and board. He says he's getting too old for farm work and the like and wants me to help him out."

In the fall of 1988, Jack McCormick spent a little time in jail, on an old truck theft charge. He claims that he had taken the truck during one of the times he was "blacked out" by whiskey and couldn't remember any of it.

After the jail stint, he was back at the mission, and Ray Copeland talked to him about coming to work at his farm, provided Jack had a valid Missouri driver's license. McCormick got his driver's license on June 21, 1989, and started driving a van for the mission. Then, in late July, he agreed to go to work for Copeland.

On the trip to Mooresville, Copeland let McCormick drive part of the way, and stopped to phone ahead to his wife to let her know he'd found a new hired hand.

Jack's curiosity about Copeland also surfaced during the trip to the Copeland farm. McCormick had seen Copeland at the mission over the past few months, and had wondered about the fate of some of the men he'd hired.

One in particular, known only as "R.C.," was a traveling buddy of McCormick's and he'd left with Ray several weeks earlier, never to be seen again.

"What ever happened to R.C.?" Jack asked.

"Had to go see his mother in California," was Ray's terse reply.

Jack thought to himself: R.C. was always talking about his mother, but he said she lived in Memphis.

At the yellow farm house, Ray Copeland didn't want any wasted time. Faye had dinner ready, and Jack McCormick was told to get his stuff stashed away. He wanted to get out early the next morning to get going on the cattle sale business.

Faye helped McCormick get settled in a small bedroom down a hallway from the Copelands', but told him he'd have to stash his stuff under the bed or somewhere, because the closet was full. McCormick later took a look at the closet and found it was full of men's clothing in a variety of sizes, colors, and styles, hanging on the crossbar or stacked on the floor.

After a meal of beef stew, Ray explained the operation to Jack. McCormick had just enough con man in him to realize that something was not quite right, but it didn't bother him. He was a stranger, a complete unknown, and that was fine with him.

The next day, with Copeland at the wheel, the pair drove the twenty or so miles to Brookfield. First, McCormick opened a post office box at the Brookfield post office, after Copeland warned him: "Don't tell them you know me."

Then they went down the street just a half block to the United Missouri Bank, and opened a checking account. Ray Copeland fished two hundred dollars from the wallet in his bib overall pockets and gave Jack McCormick his seed money.

With a pad of blank checks in hand, Jack McCormick walked back across the street to the Copeland pickup, and was told to sign one of the blank checks and give it to Ray Copeland: "In case we get killed, my wife can get the money out of the account."

During the period before the printed checks were delivered, the two men attended a number of cattle sales. Copeland would drop McCormick off a few hundred yards from the sale barn, and they would not be seen together any time during the sale. Ray Copeland was looking for four hundred- to six hundred-pound cows, in lots of about a dozen or so.

In early August, the checks came, and Ray Copeland fronted Jack an additional nine hundred dollars for the account.

Copeland had learned to be more careful with the transients . . . and their bank accounts from two earlier bad experiences.

Most of the cattle auction barn owners knew one another, and were frequently in touch about problems or big buyers working the sales. They also compared notes on credit problems or bad checks, and the word was getting out that sizeable checks written by strangers were bouncing all the way back from the bank, and law authorities weren't able to find the check-writers.

The barn owners were becoming more cautious.

Several years earlier, Copeland had showed up in Brunswick, Missouri, at Don Meyer's sale barn, with a young man named Pitts. According to Don Meyer, young Pitts attempted to buy $14,000 worth of cattle, after overbidding for the critters, and Meyer balked at accepting the check. "Old Ray Copeland just stepped right in and said 'That boy's money is good. I've known him for years,' " Meyer remembers.

But Meyer was still nervous, phoned the bank, and found out the check was not covered by deposits in the account, and refused to take it. Don Meyer's nephew, Phillip Meyer, said Pitts aroused suspicion because of his careless, high bidding, and because he was young and sported a number of racy tattoos. "He just didn't look right," young Meyer recalls.

Just who Pitts was is not known, but the failure of the scam had taught Ray Copeland a valuable lesson. Exorbitant bids aroused too much suspicion.

Another young man Ray Copeland hired didn't work out, but the man survived by his wits and road smarts. Luther Borner was born in East Germany, his mother eventually married an American GI stationed in West Germany, and the family later was stationed at massive Fort Leonard Wood, Missouri, until divorce scattered things again.

Luther Borner ended up in Texas and

other places, and started having trouble with the bottle and had frequent run-ins with the law. He had worked as a truck driver, tire changer, and day laborer. In 1986, he signed up with a circus and tented through thirty-eight states before ending the work in 1988 and landing at the Souls Harbor Mission in Joplin.

After landing in Joplin, about an hour away from Ray Copeland's other frequent stop in Springfield, Luther Borner found work at the Joplin Stockyards and married. On Labor Day, 1989, because the stockyards were closed, Luther Borner met Ray Copeland at the mission, where he occasionally worked at the front counter. Ray Copeland introduced himself to Luther Borner as Mr. Jones, and explained that he was deaf and needed help on his farm and with buying and selling cattle. Borner shouted his answers to Ray Copeland's questions, and reacted favorably to Ray Copeland's promise of fifty dollars a day, plus room and board, seven days a week, whether they worked or not.

Luther Borner eagerly told Ray Copeland he wanted the job, and was about to leave with the farmer, when Copeland found out Borner was married, and that seemed to sour the deal. "No, no, can't take you," Copeland told Borner. "Can't have no family guy, no family problems, too much work to do."

Copeland left the mission, telling Borner he'd be back in a week or so, and asked the man to look for others who might be interested in the job. A few days later Ray was back, and Luther again expressed interest in working for Copeland. "My marriage is rocky at best, and I can do the job for you, Mr. Jones," Luther Borner said.

Copeland relented, asked Luther how long it would take him to pack, and Borner, with his clothes in two plastic trash bags, headed to Chillicothe with Copeland. On the way north, Ray Copeland explained the usual routine: Cattle would be bought in Luther Borner's name, after he opened a post office box and checking account.

"Why in my name?" Borner asked.

"My credit's not too swift," Copeland answered.

Faye Copeland was with Ray Copeland as they took Luther Borner to the farm, and the couple quizzed him about cattle, asking him to identify cattle and machinery as they passed farms. Ray also quizzed him repeatedly about his family life, where his mother lived, if he had brothers and sisters, was he sure the marriage was over.

"Forget about your wife," Ray told him.

"We got a lot of work to do."

After getting to the Copeland farm late at night, Ray Copeland and Luther Borner were out shortly after first light the next morning, out to get the address established at a post office and get the checking account opened. Ray pointed out sale barns as they drove around, repeating the pattern they'll use. They went to nearby Waverly, Missouri, and opened a post office box; Ray Copeland fished the money from his wallet in his overall flap pocket.

The bank, however, balked at opening an account because of the skimpy address, and an angry Ray Copeland headed toward Chillicothe. The pair succeeded in opening an account at the First State Bank, catty-corner from the courthouse in Chillicothe.

"There's a sucker born every minute!" Copeland laughed as he learned Luther Borner had opened the account.

The next day, however, Luther Borner was puzzled and then frightened to see mail lying on the kitchen table in the Copeland home: It was addressed to Ray Copeland . . . there was no "Mr. Jones" after all.

Luther Borner's suspicions were increasing. Like most of the men who worked for the Copelands, he had sensed there was some kind of scam afoot, but after having been down as long as these men had, skirting around the law and the banks was not considered particularly suspect.

Borner, a muscular, hard-eyed young man with a more-than-frequent burst of temper, confronted Ray Copeland. "Your name ain't Jones, it's Copeland," Luther says, and Ray Copeland tried to explain, but not to Luther Borner's satisfaction.

"I want back to Joplin, I want you to take me back down to the mission right now," Luther Borner demanded.

Before Luther Borner ever had a chance to take part in the scheme, Ray had delivered him back to Joplin.

Jack McCormick also proved to be a difficult employee also, and things started moving faster than either man could keep up with.

By the second day of his employment at the Ray Copeland farm, Jack McCormick got in trouble with Faye. The elderly couple had been napping, Jack McCormick remembers, and he decided to take a walk out on the forty-acre Copeland farm. He walked down toward a small pond behind the house, and suddenly saw Mrs. Copeland running toward him, shouting that he shouldn't walk around on the farm.

The first real venture into cattle buying was a bust, with a planned major purchase in Sedalia, Missouri, falling through when Jack McCormick was outbid.

Both Copelands were mad at him over the failed purchase, and Jack McCormick began to think it was time for him to move on. He told the Copelands he was quitting.

"He ain't worth a shit as a cattle buyer," Copeland told his wife.

Nonetheless, a few purchases were made over the next few days.

On August 10, "everything came crashing down," Jack McCormick remembered later. The Copelands got him out of bed at 5:00 A.M., and Faye left for Chillicothe on a shopping trip. Jack began gathering his belongings, and sensed Ray was more than a little angry with him.

Copeland finally came into the house, and asked Jack McCormick to come outside with him.

"Got a 'coon in the barn, need your help in getting him," Ray Copeland said. Copeland was carrying an ancient-looking lever-action .22 rifle.

So, just as it was getting light, the two

men headed to the barn, with a frightened McCormick noticing a tractor parked near the barn. A small flat trailer was hitched to the tractor, and it held a roll of black plastic sheeting and a shovel.

Jack McCormick was scared to death by this point, and kept looking over his shoulder at Copeland five feet behind him, rifle in hand. Copeland showed McCormick where the raccoon was supposedly holed up, and asked him to poke around for the critter. He handed Jack a two-foot-long stick to prod the raccoon. "I'll shoot it if you flush it out," Copeland said.

McCormick had sensed a scam when he hooked up with Copeland, a scam that he had hoped would net both men some cash. But he had figured out the punch line: The only person who was going to benefit by the check-writing scam was Ray Copeland, and the only person who wasn't going to be around to spend any of the money was Jack McCormick. That was not McCormick's notion of a good idea.

Jack McCormick figured it was time to bail out.

"Ray, I'm getting out of here, I'm quitting, I'm going on," Jack McCormick told the old man. "You got to get me to Brookfield, or I'm going to hitchhike, right now."

Ray reluctantly agreed, sensing that this whole deal with Jack McCormick was over. Copeland should have known better: Jack McCormick was older than the other men he had hired, he had a known history of near-classic booze binges, and he was the only worker who understood the check-writing operation.

McCormick wanted to go to Brookfield, twenty miles east of Chillicothe, and about forty minutes from the Copeland farm, to recover the cash in that checking account that had his name on it but contained Copeland's cash. He wanted to have a little money to get out of town with, to buy a pint of something, somewhere. Jack McCormick figured Ray Copeland owes him fifty dollars a day wages, plus a little for the wear and tear of thinking he was going to be killed.

But McCormick already had traveling money, about two thousand dollars, hidden in one of the socks he's wearing. It was his part of a small inheritance after his father's death.

McCormick quickly armed up a few of his belongings from the small bedroom in the Copeland house, tossed them into Ray Copeland's truck, and the pair headed off, passing through Chillicothe first, along Highway 36, a two- and four-lane route that bisects the state east and west.

Jack McCormick was not sure why the next stop is at the Livingston County courthouse in Chillicothe, where he sees Faye Copeland, who appeared startled to see him. She said that she was headed to an Amish community gift shop north of town, and asked Jack to come along, but he refused. McCormick then left the Copeland truck, and ambled through the courthouse, out a side door, only to run back into Ray Copeland, who's still offering him a ride.

Jack was scared almost witless by this time, and tried again to walk around the square and down a side street to avoid Ray, only to see the hulking farmer waiting for him in the pickup truck. McCormick asked again to go to Brookfield, and Copeland agreed, and they headed back away from the town square on the way east to Brookfield.

For most of the trip, McCormick sat silently, the hum of the mud tires on the concrete slab of Highway 36 was the only sound heard.

Once in Brookfield, he turned off Main, pulled into the parking lot of the Howard's Grocery, just across the street from the Kansas City-based United Missouri Bank. The modernistic building had a doorway right in Copeland's vision, and another side doorway that exited in front of the fire department and city hall and police station complex.

Jack McCormick got out, entered the bank, his usual gift of gab continuing at the teller window being worked by Jewell Phillips. "Things haven't worked out, and I need to close out this account," Jack McCormick told her. He was dressed in clothes acquired at the Victory Mission: a neat-looking sports jacket, a pair of not-quite matching slacks, and shoes that almost fit. He had his ready smile, however, and the near-constant spiel and constant eye contact that had worked so well for him in his years on the streets.

Ms. Phillips, after checking the computer screen behind her, tells him there's $139.27 in the account, and she worked on preparing the forms for him to close out the account.

McCormick, increasingly nervous about returning to Ray Copeland's truck, suddenly blurted out, "I don't want to get back in that truck." He got no reaction from Phillips. He added, "Here's the license number, you might want to keep it."

Jewell watched Jack wander toward the side door at this point, the cash in his hand. As she tossed the license number away, he veered toward the basement of the bank, which contains small meetings rooms and rest rooms, but no exit.

McCormick finally came back upstairs and heads back to Copeland's truck across the street.

Jewell looked up again. Jack, a bewildered look replacing his previous self-confident strut, paused at the counter in the center of the bank, nervously peering around, and seemed to busy himself with paperwork at the counter. Jewell Phillips became increasingly concerned about his actions, and quietly slipped to the back of her teller cage and called the police station just across the street.

"There's a guy in here really acting kinda weird," she told the dispatcher. "He might be somebody you'd want to check out, seems to me."

As she made the call, McCormick left by the side door, went around behind the bank, across the asphalt parking lot and down a dingy alley backing the Main Street storefronts.

He looked for a liquor store, a safe haven, something. It was not yet 10:00 A.M., and McCormick's thoughts were back to street smart. "I've got to get out of here, far away from here, and soon," he told himself.

Ambling farther south, he crossed under the Burlington Northern underpass that crosses atop Main Street, and spied his escape: The Helm Street Inn, with Bud and Coors neon signs in its window, just a few yards from the tracks, just off Main Street, and near a strip of abandoned buildings, grain elevators, and a large used and new car lot.

Inside the Helm Street Inn, Jack McCormick is back in his element. A thirty-foot bar bisects the old establishment, running almost directly to the doorway. The back bar has the usual food listings (hamburgers, strip steaks, oyster stew) and a triple shelf of liquor bottles near the beer taps. The bar, a varnished particleboard affair with purple elbow rests, is fronted by light colored sculptured carpet. There was only one customer at the bar and a pair of regulars at a wooden table within easy reach of the bar. There's a homemade sign Scotch-taped to the refrigerator at the end of the back bar, an appliance used to keep popular frozen candy bars rockhard, and for some of the food and drinks used in the bar. The sign should have alerted McCormick to what he was getting into: "Mo Bartenders See More Assholes Than

Doctors Do." The sign is just above a list of several dozen names under the heading: No more tabs until paid.

McCormick's street smarts enabled him to size up the place rapidly, quickly spotting the owner-bartender Bill Olinger leaning against the back bar nursing a Diet Coke. Taking a seat at the bar, Jack ordered up a shot of vodka and water, and began to relax again. He was clear of Copeland, back in his element, now it was time to swing back in action.

The spiel began: "Needing to rent a car for a couple of days, then I'll be heading to Vegas, back home," Jack McCormick told Olinger, as he ordered up a second round of vodka.

"He's just a typical bullshitter," Olinger remembers thinking to himself, "kinda like you run into in a place like this, especially before noon." But McCormick was paying for his pleasure, keeping a stack of cash and change atop the bar, as he continued to run his patter.

Erma Nickel, a cook for the Helm Street Inn, had taken a break before the usual noontime crunch started.

Having fixed herself a drink, she stood behind the bar, a vacant look in her eyes as she prepared for work. Jack McCormick started in on her: "You look like you could use a break," McCormick said, a broad smile crossing his face. He was rolling now, feeling more like Jack McCormick. "Why, I just oughta take you to Vegas with me, you know? You wanta go with me . . . I'll be leaving in a couple of days . . . gotta rent a car first for some business here, and then off to the airport and out to Vegas. Got a great place there, and, well, you know about Vegas, don't you? We could have a big ol' time."

Erma Nickel payed little attention, sloughing off the pitch just like she would with anyone who started in with this kind of nonsense.

"There's a guy eats in here most every day from down the street and he rents cars," Olinger told McCormick. "His name is Harry Wolfe and he oughta be in here in a minute. He's usually got cars he rents, does it quite a bit as a matter of fact. Maybe you oughta talk to him."

"Point him out for me when he comes in, will you?" McCormick asked.

Shortly after 12:00 P.M., as is his usual routine, Harry Wolfe ambled up to the Helm Street Inn for his usual burger and Coke.

The dealership, featuring new Chevrolets and GBOs and a tacky assortment of well-used cars, is only a block and a half away, and Harry Wolfe had managed to make more than a few car deals over lunch at the popular eatery.

Taking a seat at a table away from the bar, Wolfe waited for his food when Olinger pointed him out for McCormick.

Jack McCormick started his spiel again and set his sights on Harry Wolfe. "Harry, you old sonofagun, how you getting along these days . . . haven't seen you in a while," he started out.

Most car salesmen have just a touch of larceny in their system, and the good-humored Harry Wolfe is certainly no exception. He paused only briefly in the thought that he was not sure he'd ever seen this smiling man taking a seat at his table, a drink in hand.

"I've had open heart surgery since you saw me last, but, man, I'm doing just fine, and I need me a cheap car, to rent or maybe buy," McCormick started out, the mark maybe easier than he thought. "Ever since I got out of the embalming business, been spending more and more time flying, and now I'm needing just cheap transportation from the airport to my place, y'know? Don't want something just parked here when I'm gone that some knot-head would steal, y'know? Just need something that'll run and get me back and forth, sometimes five or six times a month, sometimes less than that. Kinda depends on my schedule and the weather, stuff like that."

Wolfe, hungry but not one to pass a sales possibility after thirty-eight years in the car business, mumbled through his food that he's got just the car for Jack McCormick, an old Ford Pinto that he could buy for $495.

"Finish up, Harry, and we'll go take a look," Jack said, finding this whole scene easier than he thought.

Walking back to the car lot, past the new cars and the newer used cars, Harry Wolfe and Jack McCormick were soon in the back lot full of clunkers and rusted out old cars that still have a solid market in this economically depressed region.

"Here she be," Harry Wolfe said to Jack McCormick, pointing out the old Pinto. "I'll go get the keys and you take a look around."

Jack McCormick didn't need to look around. Harry Wolfe was back in a minute with the keys, unlocked the Pinto and cranked it to life. "Hasn't been started for a few days, but she'll run, just fine," Harry said with the resolve of a shoe salesman trying to convince a customer with a size seven foot that the size six shoe will soon relax and be perfectly comfortable.

Jack McCormick acted stubborn and walked around the crate, appearing to be looking closely at the rust spots and dents on the car. "Tell you what, Harry, I'll try it first, but think I'd be ready to give you four hundred dollars right now for it."

Wolfe flipped the car keys to McCormick, and said, "Take her for a spin, Jack, and see what you think. We can make a deal, you betcha."

As Jack McCormick puttered past the new cars through the muddy gravel drive and back out on Helm Street, Harry Wolfe was still trying to figure out where he knew McCormick from.

Chapter Seven

"Oh man! I'm outta here," Jack McCormick recalls shouting out loud, smacking the heel of his hand on the well-worn steering wheel of the roaring, sputtering Pinto. He headed down Brookfield's Helm Street, hangs a right on Main Street, toward his lone reference marker of the area, Highway 36. By now, knowing that he was clear of Ray Copeland and Harry Wolfe, McCormick started worrying about his belongings still left at the Copeland farm. He was ready for more vodka and a place to rest.

Heading back west on Missouri 36, Jack McCormick goes back to Chillicothe, his thoughts now quickly focused on a room, booze, and a way to get back his stuff. It had been a long time since McCormick had just totally dumped his belongings, and he didn't plan to start that action again. He'd managed to pull together a pretty impressive array of possessions in the past several

115

months, and he didn't want to just leave it all at the Copeland farm.

He knows he's got a few hours before Wolfe's growing concerns about his old, used Pinto will turn into action. McCormick knows that soon enough Wolfe will get the police scouting around for the car, but in the meantime he's got time to plot his next actions.

At 4:30 P.M. that afternoon, Harry Wolfe knew he'd been clipped. He called the Brookfield police, and while waiting for an officer to take down his report of the missing clunker of a car, Wolfe stared out the car dealership window. "He's good, he's real good," he said, a backhanded, if angry, compliment to the aging but still pretty sharp skills of Jack McCormick.

Jack has already checked into the Capri Motel, a small unit in a cluster of motels at the intersection of Highways 36 and 65 at the southern edge of Chillicothe. He recalls his thinking at the time.

"They might be looking, at least around Brookfield, for his car by now," he warned himself, "and I better not use it to go back out to the Copelands. Ah well, something will work out . . . let's find a place to get something to drink."

Finding a nearby tavern, McCormick quickly struck up a conversation with regular customer Rose Clevenger, unloading a new spiel about being a construction worker who'd been working out at Ray Copeland's farm. He'd quit the job, he said convincingly, and needed someone to take him back out to the farm to get his belongings.

The offer of fifty dollars quickly convinced Rose Clevenger to cooperate, and soon the newly met pair headed west toward Mooresville and the Copeland farm, Jack McCormick continuing his ever-growing, booze-fed, line of bullshit.

They arrive at the farm. Ray was not home, but Faye angrily greeted them when they walk up on the front porch, chiding McCormick out for being a lousy, drunken employee and for leaving them in a lurch. An obviously angry Faye Copeland makes a point of copying down Rose Clevenger's license number. Jack McCormick gets the rest of his things, and the pair headed back to Chillicothe and another drink.

McCormick's memory of the next several hours is a bit of a blur. He professes to have a long history of what he terms "blackouts," periods while he's drinking heavily when he has no memory of what's taken place. It's been a convenient alibi for him over the years, but is at least partially true, given his history with the bottle.

He left Chillicothe, either later that night, or the next morning, and headed south on Highway 65, in the general direction of his mother's home in Lebanon, Missouri.

He remembers being there for a couple of days, possibly drying out, and probably trying to reassure his aging mother (who was about at her wit's end with his long history of troubles and travels). Then he left the "hot" Pinto and got behind the wheel of another car, borrowed from his mother and started heading north and west, passing very few bars along the way.

It was late August, and his three weeks with the Copelands was beginning to blend in with all his other jobs and travails. He veered northwest out of Missouri, taking the Interstate across Nebraska, hoping possibly to find work at his old carnival company or other short-term work somewhere along the way. In Nebraska he decided, for reasons still not quite clear, to phone the Nebraska CrimeStoppers hot line. Stopping at an Interstate rest area, McCormick nervously dials the number and spews out his claim of seeing bodies on the Copeland farm, including a skull and leg bone. He told the officers he'd seen murders and mayhem on the farm. He indicated that Ray Copeland had killed four workers over the past several months. It was 7:30 P.M., August 20, 1989 and Officer Carey dutifully copied down the incredible story. Jack McCormick didn't identify himself and continued in a drunken stupor west.

McCormick maintains to this day that he called and told his story out of an interest in truth and justice. As a longtime veteran street person, it could well be that Jack McCormick had indeed been concerned about the welfare of his fellow travelers. He'd grown to know these men and boys, and felt a certain kinship, and even a fatherly responsibility toward them. Others argue he may have been trying to shift attention from his own wrongdoings (the bad checks, written and yet to come) to the Copelands or maybe even trying to extract a little revenge against the old farmer who'd pointed a rifle at his head. The real truth of it is forever lost in an alcoholic haze somewhere along the highways.

Jack was back in his element now, on the road, on what he would often refer to as a "rolling drunk." He knew the routine well.

With a badly overdrawn checking account and post office box address from some unknown small town in Missouri, Jack McCormick was able to cash check after check, for everything from gasoline to groceries, and even whiskey now and again.

Deputy Gary Calvert was "tracking" Jack McCormick's trip west with the help of the United Missouri Bank in Brookfield. When they'd get checks back and not pay them, the bank would let Calvert know the location. While Calvert didn't know it was Jack McCormick who'd made that call to the Nebraska hotline, he was beginning to suspect it may have been him, and dearly wanted to talk to the man.

Gary Calvert's involvement in the Copeland case was becoming nearly an obsession with him, and he knew that talking to someone who had been involved in the check-writing schemes was a key. So far, the tracing of the checks and cattle purchases had been by paper only. He'd talked to no one who'd been involved in any of the deals, and was now basically getting nowhere talking to the Copelands and their family. Whoever this Jack McCormick was was a key to the case, because it was a still-living person associated with bad checks and linked to Ray and Faye Copeland. The checks—and McCormick— were obviously going to become a key item in this growing investigation and Gary Calvert knew it.

Back at the Copeland farm, there was another occupant of the spare bedroom. The day after Jack McCormick left the house, Ray Copeland went back to Springfield, Missouri, back to the Victory Mission, and talked another man into coming to work for him.

But in his apparent growing desperation, Copeland had gotten less selective about whom he hired. While he originally had sought out young men without families, men who hopefully had somewhat of a farm background and who could help pull off the scam at the sale barns, he was now hiring just about anyone who would agree to leave with him.

Jimmy Page, fifty-years-old, disabled, and unemployed, was near the mission, standing on a small footbridge over a creek smoking a cigarette. Ray Copeland drove up in his pickup, leaned out the window, and asked Page if he'd like to earn fifty dollars a day driving a truck.

Jimmy jumped at the offer and within an

hour was off to Chillicothe and Mooresville. That night, Jimmy was settled in at the Copeland home, his clothes crowded in alongside the leftover clothes of men now dead and buried. Copeland had explained to Page on their way to the farm that he needed help at cattle auctions because he was going deaf and couldn't hear the auctioneer's cry.

The two opened a post office box and checking account and started attending cattle sales over a wide area of Missouri. Ray Copeland gave Page two thousand dollars, a huge sum for the drifter, and he watched through the bank window as Page opened the account.

"He told me he would nudge me in the back with his knee when he wanted me to bid," Page remembers. He wasn't allowed to smoke in the Copeland house and was told not to use the Copeland telephone or address for any correspondence. "They didn't want some of my relatives knowing where I was," Jimmy said. The Copelands did see to it that he was fed and housed, and even told him he could fish in their pond.

Ray traveled to Chillicothe one day with Jimmy and bought him a pair of overalls. "So I'd look more like a farmer," Page recalls.

The scheme was set, and Page was uniformed and ready. The timing of his arrival at the Copeland farm likely saved his life.

A startled, scared Jimmy Page was at the Copeland farm when the law officers closed in with a search warrant and started scouring for bodies that day in October.

The check charges that he already amassed were dropped, and Jimmy Page filled officers in on what he knew. He shuddered when he heard what they thought had happened to his predecessors.

Jimmy Page went back — gladly — to Springfield.

"I think I was being set up," Page said.

Chapter Eight

Gary Calvert first sensed something was amiss as early as 1986.

He'd been a deputy in Livingston County for about five years when the first sale barn contacted the sheriff's office. Prior to that, he'd worked three years in neighboring Carroll County, and before that had been a detective with the Tucson, Arizona police department. Today he laughs at his determination to leave Tucson and get back to rural Missouri so he could be clear of the major crimes striking the growing Arizona community. "Thought I'd find peace and quiet back here," he says, a wry smile breaking his usually solemn expression.

He was seldom directly involved in handling bad checks in his job as chief deputy for the Livingston County sheriff's office. Bad checks in this county often meant a twelve dollar insufficient funds check to the Amoco Food Shop for a tank of gas, or a small check for groceries at the United Super.

The bad checks eventually (after the writers were given chance after chance to right the bad paper) showed up in Associate Circuit Judge Barbara Lame's courtroom in the Livingston County courthouse, where she lectured and cajoled, usually to blank eyes and earnest promises.

The checks that had been landing on Deputy Calvert's desk, however, weren't the usual multi-punched and stamped insufficient funds checks that are a constant nuisance for rural county sheriff's offices.

He thumbed through the checks, noting the cattle barns and the sometimes near illiterate scrawl from the check-writer.

Who on earth wrote these things? Who in the world is Jimmie Harvey? Paul Cowart?

In this county of fifteen thousand residents, lawmen like Calvert know just about everybody, especially those who repeatedly drop bad paper around town. Many times the frequent bad check-writers are denied banking privileges. Then they begin being cash-only customers around the county, and the problems cease.

In his patient, methodical style, Calvert

had snooped around, asking questions at the sale barns, bringing up the names at Pam's Cafe, or when he'd stop and chat with farmers as he patrolled the rural stretches of the county. He was usually surprised at how few people seemed to know much about the man who'd authored the bad checks. In his years as a deputy around Livingston County, he'd usually found that some of his regular contacts always seemed to know about everyone else. Once in a while he'd heard Ray Copeland's name, that maybe "old Ray" was hiring drifters and unknowns to work for him, and that maybe they'd been passing the checks. But that was about it. And, it was not unusual for elderly farmers, or young ones for that matter, to hire young men for temporary work. Sometimes the hands were not local youngsters, many of whom were more willing to wear a paper hat and fry potatoes than take on the hard and dirty work of helping farmers.

Strangers aren't unnoticed for very long in a rural county like Livingston, and everyone's vehicle is pretty well-known. If "old Ray" was seen driving around with a stranger, an outsider if you will, it was known around the area. And, despite the fact that Copeland was starting to travel farther and farther from home for sales and banks and post offices, most farmers are fairly mobile, especially in the off-crop seasons. They often think nothing of driving forty or fifty miles for a cattle sale or farm auction.

Yet, while the studious-looking Gary Calvert was methodically gathering this information, there still wasn't much he could do with it, other than mentally file it away. There was no law against hiring help; there was no law against being a bum; there was no law against associating with somebody up to no good. He had learned in the investigation that Copeland had been involved in a bad check scheme in Ozark County a decade and a half earlier, and he'd pulled up the computer records showing the old man had a string of check and fraud charges and convictions. But nowhere in Ray Copeland's file was any indication of violence against anyone.

Calvert just kept piling little bits of information together, trying to make sense of it all. He also was tracking the men who wrote the checks; finding they'd let driver's licenses lapse; they'd not been in contact with family members; apparently they'd dropped out of sight.

Even the most downtrodden of the transients, even the guys who'd fought and lost the most battles with booze, usually had someone they stayed in contact with. Deputy Calvert, like many other law enforcement officers beginning to tiptoe into this case, had long assumed that many of the drifters they'd run into over the years had totally dropped out. He was a little surprised, and perhaps even a little relieved, to find out that instead many had at least one safe harbor, one place they could still go back to and perhaps not face days of lecture and complaints. Once those locations were found, Calvert began to piece together somewhat sketchy, but revealing, pictures of the missing men.

It was this kind of thoroughness and thinking that had earned Gary a reputation for being a good lawman. Livingston County Prosecuting Attorney Doug Roberts said Calvert was one of the few local officers who could present information about a case and never leave him wondering how accurate and thorough it really was. Most officers had to turn in detailed, written reports about alleged crimes to Roberts; Calvert could usually pass on verbal reports and Roberts would feel comfortable enough to file charges.

The kick-down-the-door-style cops of television fame aren't usually found in the rural Midwest. The successful cops are plodding, resourceful, and often just plain lucky. And they know many people who like to talk, and to gossip and snoop. Most "confessions" aren't forced out of suspects: The suspects simply just keep talking and talk themselves right into trouble.

Calvert, lean and intense-looking, often wore a business suit rather than a deputy's uniform. His heavy dark glasses, soft voice, and comfortable smile allowed him on the good side of many a bad guy over the years. Outlaws would suddenly find themselves telling this deputy sheriff things they shouldn't really be talking about. Gary Calvert liked being a cop.

If he harbored political aspirations for Sheriff O'Dell's job, he mostly kept them to himself. He knew that if that was ever going to work out, it would be in due time. The sheriff's job is still a political plum in rural counties, with a good salary and ample respect. It's often on the minds of deputies and town police officers, and it's not unusual for members of the prestigious Missouri State Highway Patrol to give up their blue uniform for the brown uniform of a sheriff, or at least to secretly harbor the notion.

Realistically, Leland O'Dell was a good politician and had, for the most part, been a pretty good sheriff. He would not be a snap to defeat.

But the primary thing on Gary Calvert's mind these days was that he still liked being a cop, and he wondered what old Ray Copeland was up to and where all this was going to lead.

At least initially, he figured Ray Copeland's involvement in the bad check scheme was well short of murder. Calvert figured that the rough old farmer was setting these unknown guys up, then paying them off and sending them on their way. Murder—brutal execution with a single shot in the back of the head—was not thought to be part of the operation here. There would be little need, Calvert reasoned, to do anything but give these guys a little money or a bottle of booze and send them on their way. These guys weren't really a threat to Ray Copeland, Calvert thought, and there would be little reason to execute them.

But, the further Gary Calvert got into this case, and the more dead ends he ran into, he certainly wasn't ruling out the brutal possibilities, either.

Prosecuting Attorney Doug Roberts usually had several legal irons in the fire, and disliked many of them. As a five-term prosecuting attorney in Livingston County, Roberts never ceased to be surprised at some of the people he had to deal with: thugs and low-lifes, child beaters and wife beaters, those barely literate and those smart enough to have stayed out of trouble.

Roberts had left his hometown of Chillicothe for the University of Michigan law school in Ann Arbor, receiving his law degree and coming back to a law practice in Kansas City, two hours from his old hometown. He later practiced law in nearby Gallatin, Missouri, getting his first taste of county seat politics and law practice. Then, after marrying, he settled back in Chillicothe in 1976, a thirty-year-old lawyer ready for a political future.

He was unopposed in his first shot at the Livingston County prosecutor's job in 1976 and kept the job for a half dozen years. He got caught up in the local politics in 1982, got trounced in a reelection bid, and went back to a solo private practice. His successor, however, resigned in 1988, and Doug Roberts was then reappointed to the prosecutor's job, and elected in his own right later that same year.

By the summer of 1989, Doug Roberts, too, sensed something was coming, and he shuddered at what it might be. He knew (Gary Calvert and other police officers had kept him posted) that there was a pattern of bad checks being written at cattle auction barns by people no one had ever heard of. He knew that rumor and some eyewitness reports linked some of the check-writers to old Ray Copeland, and that some of the check-writers had been seen with the crusty old farmer he'd met years ago when creditors were closing in. And, he knew something had to give . . . and probably soon. Farmers aren't dominant in numbers here, but can be stout in political clout. If the farmers and the cattle sale barn owners began loudly grumbling that Doug Roberts couldn't . . . or wouldn't . . . prosecute bad checks bouncing through sale barns, he could be out of a job. There weren't that many lawyers in Livingston County who would be interested in running for the job of county prosecuting attorney, but Doug Roberts had learned to like the position he held. He didn't want to give it up unless it was by his own choice.

The concerns were not dominant, but on his early morning visits to the Northside

Cafe across from the courthouse, or at Pam's, a block farther from the courthouse, Roberts wondered about the strange Copeland case. What in the world is that gruff old farmer up to? Why can't we get a break here?

Sullivan County, a county of some 6,800 residents at the northeast edge of Livingston County, is Sheriff Bill Hayes's turf. He was holding some bad paper written to the Milan Livestock Market and a similar market in Green City by one Jack McCormick. Hayes had quickly issued a warrant for McCormick and had entered him into the national computer of people wanted by law agencies. Like his cohorts in Livingston County, Hayes had never heard of McCormick, surprising in a county this small.

His county, like others in the area, had been hit by the Ray Copeland-led bad check scams over the past several months. Sheriff Hayes was sick of it, and was working with livestock barn owners and others to see if he could get it stopped. Sometimes he was tempted to lecture the sale barn owners on the lack of identification and accounting that was involved in taking a large check from someone they'd never seen or heard of. But, he usually backed off on the sermons and just tried to solve the cases.

Secretly, he had little hope that this McCormick fellow, whoever he was, would ever surface again.

Jack McCormick, however, ran out of luck, money, and real estate on September 13, 1989, in Salem, Oregon. He didn't have a car anymore, he was nearly broke, and he'd been blind drunk for weeks. His mind was a blank as to much of what had happened since he'd left Missouri.

When Jack McCormick left the Copeland farm and eventually left Missouri, he had had his share of the money from the estate of his late father. The cash was kept in one of his shoes, and was apparently spent joyously as he traveled toward the setting sun. He left Missouri with that cash, and, of course, the handy (and worthless) checking account from the United Missouri Bank in Brookfield. He must have lived pretty high across the prairies. He had no money and was out of checks when he was finally apprehended.

When he was found, he was "camped" alongside a road near Salem, Oregon, basically just sprawled out alongside the highway. Oregon officers stopped and checked him out, the usual sort of procedure for transients along the highways these days. After routine entries in the national crime information computer data banks, it was learned Jack McCormick was wanted in Sullivan County, Missouri, for writing a two thousand dollar bad check at the Green City Livestock Market.

The word was sent back to Sullivan County, and Sheriff Bill Hayes was surprised to hear back from his warrant. McCormick waived extradition and agreed to return to Missouri on September 15. Jack was at his talkative best in the Oregon jail, drawing a crude, but reasonably accurate, sketch of the Copeland house. He even put together a rough map of the Copeland farm, marking spots where he claimed he'd seen bodies. His maps, along with a copy of the Oregon police report and other comments made by McCormick, came back to Missouri with him.

In general discussions during the months preceding his discovery of McCormick, Bill Hayes and Livingston County authorities had talked about the bad checks and Ray Copeland. They felt that something was connected and something was going to have to break in one of these cases. A couple of livestock barn owners told Hayes they just somehow knew Ray Copeland was involved in all this, and that they would tear up the bad checks and forget about retrieving the loss if something could be pinned on the old Mooresville farmer. It was worth ending the string of bad checks, even if they had to take a loss, they figured.

Before Sheriff Hayes went to Oregon, he sat down with Livingston County authorities, and Livingston County Deputy Gary Calvert told Hayes about their suspicions concerning Copeland. They added that Jack McCormick might have the missing piece to the multi-state puzzle.

Calvert had an Oregon police officer interrogate McCormick before Sheriff Hayes got there, and asked him about the Nebraska phone call, which Jack McCormick quickly said he'd made at about 7:30 P.M. on August 20, 1989.

"We figured this could lead to something," Bill Hayes says about the trip to Oregon.

Two days after Jack McCormick agreed to return to Missouri, Hayes and a guard flew to Portland, drove to Salem, and met a character they'll likely never forget.

"He acted like he'd known us twenty years," Sheriff Hayes recalls of his first meeting with McCormick. "You'd a'thought we were old buddies . . . I'd never laid eyes

137

on him before that."

Jack McCormick had sobered up in the Oregon jail and now knew that he had to stay sharp and work a deal in his Copeland connection. He also knew that he had exaggerated his claims on the Nebraska phone call, particularly the part about the bodies and bones. But, in the best jail house tradition, he figured he'd worry about that later.

The handcuffed McCormick and the lawmen were barely on the airplane back to Missouri before Jack started repeating his stories about the Copelands, about the bodies and body parts he had seen on the farm, about the bad checks and the cattle buying, about Ray Copeland aiming an old .22 at him on that final day at the Copeland place. He seemed to recall clearly details from his final day at the Copeland farm, even telling officers he noticed that the safety was in the off position on Ray Copeland's .22 caliber old rifle.

Soon after the trio was back in Missouri, Hayes got in touch with Leland O'Dell and told him they sure might want to talk to Jack McCormick. During the trip from the Kansas City airport back to Milan, McCormick continued his stories, embellished with his good humor and knowledge of the area and its people. He seemingly had total recall

138

of where he'd dropped the bad checks, and had no doubt in his own mind as to how Copeland was working his scam on the market operators. And, as usual, Jack won over the usually hard-nosed sheriff with his outgoing friendliness and seemingly complete candor and honesty.

"He is a real likable fellow," Bill Hayes still says of McCormick. "You kinda figured on some of what he was telling us, he was storying a little bit, but other parts sure seemed to be right and he seemed like he knew what he was talking about."

Perched in the Sullivan County jail, Livingston County and Missouri State Highway Patrol officers quickly called on McCormick, interviewed him extensively, and came away thinking the whole Copeland thing was about to blow wide open.

They were right.

Jack McCormick, looking worse for the wear but coming back to life in jail with three squares and no booze, repeated his stories about Copeland and what had happened at the farm. For the first time, he implied Faye Copeland was involved, that she was the business brains and had been in on conversations setting up post office addresses and checking accounts.

Up to this point, most of those working on the case had only seriously considered Ray as the prime mover in the growing case.

For the next several days, officers continued to pile up information and clues about what McCormick had said and about how it tied into the Copelands. They soon saw they were developing more than enough information to go and arrest the pair and to begin a search. The almost unspoken assumption now was that the search would be for bodies.

The weekend before October 9, 1989 was a busy, frantic one for lawmen and prosecutors, all hoping to keep things quiet for a few more days.

One of their fears was that if Ray Copeland got wind of the investigation, he would have time to destroy or remove any evidence on the farm.

The conversations with McCormick were revealing and frightening, and Doug Roberts now knew he had enough information to seek a search warrant and enough to charge the Copelands with at least conspiracy to commit fraud.

On a Thursday night, Roberts, O'Dell, and Calvert met and went over what they had:

1. A stack of bad checks, with a variety of names, and only one check-writer (Jack McCormick) around to talk about them.

2. A pair of reports from relatives seeking information on men last heard from in Livingston County.

3. Eyewitness reports of Ray Copeland being seen with a variety of drifters he'd hired; men who'd lived at the farm with the Copelands, but who weren't there now.

4. And, finally, the interview with Jack McCormick, still filled with reports of bone sightings, and, more importantly, the details on how he said the cattle scam worked.

"That's enough," Roberts finally said, meaning there was enough information to seek a search warrant and arrest the Copelands.

"I think it's key that we arrest her, too," Roberts said. "She might be a little more afraid of jail than he probably is, and maybe she'll tell us something. And it looks like she may have been the record-keeper, which gets her into this thing up to her eyeballs."

The meeting (one of dozens in those secretive days) was ending, and Gary Calvert added a chilling benediction. "I've put together a list of names, people that might be involved in this, people we can't find any more, people who may have worked for the Copelands. It has a dozen names."

Doug Roberts called Associate Circuit Judge Barbara Lame, outlined what was going to happen, and set up a Monday morning meeting for the search warrant and arrest warrant for the Copelands.

Judge Lame was very careful in preparation of the search warrant, not wanting to permit a strip-mining of the Copeland farm. The search warrant had to detail the specific type of search and the goal.

"What do you think's going on here, Doug?" Judge Lame asked.

"Don't even want to think about it too much, Judge, but he may have been killing these boys."

"Oh, no, you think so?"

"Could be."

It was a Friday, and Roberts and a handful of law officers knew that Monday morning they were going to swoop down on the Copeland farm and arrest the elderly couple and scour over the farm for bodies.

That was a tough secret to keep that night.

As luck would have it, in the best mix of small town life and big-time crime, Mr. and Mrs. Roberts were among the parents who were to accompany Cub Scouts on a camp out at the local Cub Scout cabin.

Doug Roberts squirmed and was uncomfortable most of that long evening, itching to tell people about what was developing; how the airwaves and newspaper columns were going to be filled with news of the Copelands in just a few hours.

But he tended Cub Scouts instead, and kept his mouth shut.

With the business day Monday, the complaint was to be filed against the Copelands, the search warrant served, and the lid would start coming off the secret developments.

The conspiracy complaint, filed October 9, 1989, gave the public its first glimpse of the soon-to-be-unfolding Copeland case.

The complaint against both Ray and Faye Copeland read, in part:

with the purpose of promoting and facilitating the offense of stealing, agreed with Faye Copeland that they would recruit one Jack McCormick to purchase cattle on their behalf at various local livestock markets, cause the said Jack McCormick to open a Post Office box and checking account for the purchase of said cattle, where were to be transported to the farm of the (Copelands) and delivered to (the Copelands) for resale by (them), and finance the purchase of said cattle by delivering to the said Jack McCormick funds to deposit in said account, and thereafter to cause the said Jack McCormick to purchase cattle in sufficient amounts to overdraw said checking account, at which time (Copeland) would sell said cattle, retaining the proceeds thereof, and terminate the relationship with the said Jack McCormick, causing the livestock market to suffer the loss of the price to be paid by Jack McCormick; thereafter, in furtherance of the conspiracy, (Ray Copeland) Jack McCormick to open a Post Office box and checking account, delivered to the said Jack McCormick to purchase cattle, which purchase overdrafted the account of the said Jack McCormick, causing the seller to suffer a financial loss in excess of $150.

At 6:00 A.M., Monday, October 9, thirteen law enforcement officers, including Doug Roberts, met at the Livingston County jail and briefly went over the warrants and the plan and headed to the Copeland farm.

At 6:56 A.M., Deputy Gary Calvert knocked on the door of the Copeland home. He was a little apprehensive about what might lie ahead. They knew Ray Copeland had a habit of leaving home early each morning, but thought they might be early enough to catch him.

Faye Copeland came to the door, an angry but sort of confused look on her face. She was clutching a dish towel, and water was running in the kitchen sink.

"Ray here?" Calvert asked.

"Nope."

Gary Calvert was willing to bet old Ray Copeland was at Pam's Cafe having his morning coffee.

"Well, Mrs. Copeland, we've got a warrant to search your place, as part of an investigation we're working," Calvert said slowly. "And, we have a warrant for your arrest, Mrs. Copeland, on a fraud deal here."

"What you mean?" Faye Copeland said, a hint of anger in her voice.

"A search warrant, here," Calvert said, thrusting the piece of paper toward Faye. "And we'll need to place you under arrest."

"You'll have to talk to my husband," Faye said, wringing the dish towel. "He'll be right back."

Gary Calvert decided to go to Chillicothe to arrest Ray, and left two officers with Faye. The other officers, who were going to kick off the search, waited at the edge of the Copeland yard.

Pulling up at Pam's, Calvert saw Copeland's pickup and knew he was saucering his coffee inside. He quietly went inside, sat down beside Ray, and outlined the circumstances of the unexpected visit. Ray went along calmly to jail.

Deputies later escorted Faye Copeland into the jail, where she had said she needed to talk to her husband. She was officially arrested at the jail.

"Whatcha looking for on my place?" Ray Copeland asked deputies.

"Well, we're just looking for some, uh, evidence, I guess, Mr. Copeland," Calvert said. "This is all legal and all . . . here."

"Well, it's legal, then you just go ahead and search. You won't find nothing on my place."

Sheriff Leland O'Dell and two other deputies exited their patrol cars and came on toward the house, and prepared to start the search of the farm.

The searchers were already gathered up nearby, and Leland radioed them to come on to the Copeland place and get the search going.

That first day, the search was going to be primarily a surface one, with scores of deputies planning to simply walk the acreage and scour for evidence—hopefully the evidence the phone caller had said would be found. Based on what Jack McCormick had told officers, bodies should be found quickly.

It didn't work out that way.

More than two dozen officers worked on the search that first day, and found basically nothing.

That Monday night, O'Dell, Roberts, and other law officers met briefly at the jail, and decided to up the level of the efforts. They phoned local backhoe operators and contacted owners of bloodhounds.

Doug Roberts expanded the scope of the search warrant with Judge Lame.

Tuesday morning, the search intensified, and the word began to get out around the area that the searchers were looking for bodies.

The search continued. Backhoes churned

up dirt, chipped away at shallow creek banks and around tree stumps and roots, searching for remains. A six-foot-deep pit was dug in one spot near the Copelands' barn in the futile search. From a distance, reporters and photographers tried, usually in vain, to catch a glimpse of what was going on.

Doug Roberts, while not by nature or training an investigative prosecutor, joined in the searches and investigation, walking with officers and dog tenders out across the property.

Officers were puzzled and perplexed by unexplained areas on the farm where it appeared the land had been plowed and seeded, for no apparent reason. They also found scores of places where brush had been burned and where the soil had been plowed or spaded.

They found bits and pieces of bones. Roberts was nearly ecstatic one day when he found a rib bone in a burn area, but the rib had belonged to a deer likely butchered on the back acres of the farm. Other bits and pieces of bone were found, but later identified as belonging to animals other than humans.

Many of the searchers think to this day that Ray Copeland may have burned bodies and then plowed and disked the bones, leaving pieces no bigger than a dime. But they found nothing to back up those theories.

On Wednesday, with the interest in the massive search growing, and reporters finally learning some of the details, deputies brought Jack McCormick to the farm, and he spent a couple of hours trying to "remember" where he'd supposedly seen pieces of a skull and other body parts.

The people who keep the jail running for Sheriff O'Dell were ready for the Copelands. They seldom, if ever, handle people of the age of the Copelands, especially a woman. The women who are usually lodged in this jail are young toughs, tattooed ladies who are girlfriends of bad guys or who have just finally pushed the system so far they left jailers no choice but to lock them up. The jail population in a place like Livingston County is still nearly all-male and young, and is certainly seldom made up of senior citizens like Ray and Faye Copeland.

The plan was for the Copelands to be separated, for a couple of reasons. First, men and women are segregated in jails by law and practice. Secondly, officers still thought Faye Copeland was a key player in this game of seeking truth; perhaps when she had a little

149

time to peer through bars, she'd come clean with them and tell them what had been happening out on the farm.

That ended up being wishful thinking . . . as were hopes that the search was going to be a short and sweet affair.

Chapter Nine

A first time visitor to the Livingston County jail may not think they've entered the local lockup when they enter the lobby. They are greeted by a clean, spacious area, flanked by potted plants — of all things! It's only well past the double doors that the small dispatcher's "cage" becomes visible behind a glass window, the solitary spot for the dispatcher who answers the telephone calls and keeps in radio communications with the sheriff and deputies. A relatively new structure, the jail and interior offices feature none of the usual jail house smells and sights.

In the east side of the building, offices are lined up for sheriff and deputies, and there's a spacious meeting and conference room.

That area was taken over by the Northwest Missouri Major Case Squad in the days that the search opened . . . and flopped badly . . . at the Copeland farm.

The Squads are set up around the state of

Missouri to help harried local lawmen in working on major or very tough cases. They are strictly controlled, with rules and bylaws set up to establish lead investigators, assign officers to leads, and to handle the always pesky press requests.

In the days after the search opened, Leland O'Dell tried to keep the lid on the Copeland story, but to no avail. A number of Copeland neighbors were becoming regular, if unnamed, callers to the television and radio stations and newspaper offices, spreading the latest rumor or sighting of officers digging up the countryside.

O'Dell tried stonewalling, and was having trouble with the growing, news hungry press corps which was staked out around the Copeland farm and camped out at the jail.

By the second day of the search, the sheriff even tried denying that officers were searching for bodies, saying the rumors of those morbid searches were wrong, but refusing to elaborate further.

Clearly, Sheriff O'Dell welcomed the entry of the Major Case Squad and backed the squad's selection of Grundy County Sheriff Greg Coon as the press spokesman. A pleasant-natured, almost jovial young sheriff, Coon could catch the flak and get the egg on his face if the search yielded no bodies.

Ray Copeland (*back row, left*), with his mother (*back row, right*), his sister Maudie (*girl next to mother*) and various unidentified family members, circa 1930 near Harrison, Arkansas.

Ray Copeland, circa 1935.

Ray in front of his first car, circa 1938.

Faye Copeland, circa 1937.

Faye Copeland, 38, with her sons Al (*left*), Wayne (*standing*), and Sonny in front of their McClean County, Illinois home.

"Bronco Ray," circa 1942.

Ray and Sonny with a big catch in front of their McLean County, Illinois home.

Faye Copeland in the kitchen of her Mooresville home in 1967.

Ray and Faye Copeland in Chillicothe, Missouri, circa 1980.

Ray often attended local farm auctions like this one as part of his livestock scam.

Dennis K. Murphy, 27,
murdered October 17, 1986.

Wayne Robert Warner, age
unknown, murdered
November 19, 1986.

Jimmy Dale Harvey, 27,
murdered October 29, 1988.

John Wayne Freeman, 27,
murdered December 8,
1988.

Paul Jason Cowart, 21,
murdered May 1, 1989.

Livingston County Coroner Scott Lindley (*right*) leads the hunt for bodies on the Copeland farm.

Jack McCormick, the homeless man who escaped Copeland's murderous plan and alerted authorities.

The barn near Ludlow, Missouri where police discovered three bodies buried beneath the dirt floor.

Press conference announcing the five first-degree murder
charges against Ray and Faye Copeland and the state's
intention to seek the death sentence. From left to right:
Livingston County Sheriff Leland O'Dell; Missouri
Attorney General Bill Webster; Livingston County Deputy
Gary Calvert; Livingston Prosecuting Attorney Doug
Roberts; Dave Hanes and Rick Sampsel, officers in the
Northwest Missouri Major Case Squad.

Sheriff O'Dell escorts Ray Copeland in
court to be charged with the murders.

Faye Copeland after being charged
with the murders.

Ray Copeland attempted to plead guilty to avoid a death sentence. Judge E. Richard Webber refused to accept his plea.

Faye Copeland being led out of court after being convicted on all five counts of first-degree murder.

Faye and Ray Copeland await execution by lethal injection. They are the oldest couple in American criminal history to be convicted of murder and sentenced to death.

O'Dell figured he'd rather have Greg Coon out there in the jail's lobby saying, "We don't have anything" than stand out there himself saying it.

Deputy Gary Calvert and Dave Hane, a well-trained city policeman, became the chief investigators for the squad, heading up the complicated search and investigation efforts.

The squad generally used a "lead card system" that relies heavily on legwork, follow-up and thoroughness.

As each tip or telephone report would come in, an index-sized card would be filled out with the tip and the source of it, if known. For example, the card might detail a telephone report from a farmer who said Ray Copeland had once painted his barn, and had been around the farm for a few days. The card would be numbered in the order that the tip was received, and then assigned to a pair of officers.

The officers, always at least two, would then follow through on that numbered lead. They'd take card in hand, and carefully check out the tip or lead. That done, they'd write a report on their findings, a report turned in to the chief investigators, Calvert or Hane.

Calvert or Hane could accept the report from the lead card, and simply file it away with the growing stack of paper, or they could reassign the lead card to another pair of officers, hoping they'd have a different view of the tip or lead.

It was not a terribly sophisticated system, but it helped ensure that everything that came in over the telephone lines or was passed along in person was followed through.

Doug Roberts enjoyed the investigative work, spending countless hours locked up in the jail house rooms, trying to read every report and to follow through if he felt something was left unanswered. For many cops, tired of stopping motorists or checking two-bit thefts, working investigations like this was invigorating work, an exciting and challenging break from the deadly routine of day-to-day police work. There was no shortage of volunteers to work in the investigation rooms.

As usually happens when groups of cops gather on a case in small towns, the community also rallied, with boxes and sacks of food streaming into the jail hourly. Church groups would bring pies and huge thermos jugs of coffee and punch; operators of franchise fast-food joints would drop by with stacks of their goodies; pizza shop owners keep the jail lobby smelling like a slab of pepperoni. The officers ate well, and obviously enjoyed the widespread support and backing of much of the community.

The county's prosecutor also knew early on he needed help, and was in touch with the state's Attorney General's office almost from day one.

Quickly, a team of three lawyers, including young Kenny Hulshof, from Attorney General Bill Webster's Jefferson City office joined in the investigation, and subsequent trials.

Doug Roberts, despite his years as the county's prosecuting attorney, knew that his experience was limited, and he knew he'd need help if bodies started being found.

The relative quiet of Livingston County meant Roberts had never handled a homicide case; he'd never had to deal with ballistics evidence in a capital murder case; he'd never worked that extensively with forensic specialists; he'd never worked with handwriting specialists.

In short, Doug Roberts knew he'd need help and wasted no time in asking for it.

But, it was also "his" case, his prosecution

to make, and he felt confident that the out-of-town attorneys would defer to him on the public phases of the proceedings. He would be able to direct the prosecution efforts if it ever came to that.

No novice, of course, to politics, Roberts, a Democrat, knew that aggressive Republican Attorney General Bill Webster would miss no chance to make publicity hay out of the Chillicothe tragedy.

It quickly became apparent that Kenny Hulshof was going to be the Attorney General's lead attorney on the Copeland case, and Doug Roberts couldn't help but like the personable young lawyer.

The Roberts family had Hulshof over for supper a few times during the opening phases, and after the charges were filed, and enjoyed his company. Their eating area off the kitchen was the scene of long conversations about the developing case, with information and feelings freely exchanged.

Doug Roberts's wife, Diane, even takes a little credit for Kenny Hulshof's opening statement to jurors in the later Faye Copeland trial. She said one night after dinner that the whole thing read like a detective novel, and that's the approach Hulshof later took with jurors, urging them not to skip over to the last page.

The politics of a case like the Copeland tragedy may help the system work: Officers know they have to answer to the public, and the public wants results and wants criminals punished.

But politics also has a self-serving side at times.

Bill Webster was raised in politics, the son of a plain-talking and unusually powerful Republican senator in a Democratic state senate where Republicans were normally nothing much more than colorful, often crusty outsiders.

The state's highest legal position, the office of Attorney General, had become a stepping stone to higher office in modern times, thanks in part to the high-profile pro-consumer position those holding the office can often take. While governors can get bogged down with a General Assembly that could make a snail resemble an Indy racer and see their power and influence swayed by a variety of forces, the Attorney General could almost mount his white horse and charge off to protect the masses at will.

When Bill Webster was elected Attorney General in 1984, that's just what he had in mind. He established highly publicized pro-consumer hotlines, and took a strong anti-abortion stance that eventually led to a famous U.S. Supreme Court case that bears his surname, *Webster* v. *Reproductive Rights*. He argued against a family seeking to remove food and water from a severely brain-damaged daughter, and missed few chances to state his pro-death penalty stance in a state where the ultimate punishment is wildly popular.

He also had enough rural political savvy from his father that he knew to keep the local prosecutors and lawmen happy, and he established aggressive and skilled units of young lawyers to assist in high-profile land tough murder cases.

Livingston County Prosecuting Attorney Roberts had wasted little time asking for, and getting, help from Webster's office when it became obvious that the Copeland case was going to be a mammoth undertaking. Local prosecutors, especially in counties like Livingston County, seldom have budgets large enough for full-time investigators or assistant prosecutors, and a multiple-murder case or case requiring extensive investigative work will quickly overtax the local prosecutor. Roberts and secretary and assistant Charlene Coleman normally handled all the county's prosecuting business.

But Doug also quickly discovered that you get the full dose when you sign on with the Attorney General's office.

County prosecutors are proud of their legal turf and jealously guard it. If and when the state Attorney General enters the picture, historically it's been at the request of the local prosecutor and the state officials stayed on the back row. Attorney General Bill Webster, never one to shy away from publicity or press releases, jumped into the Livingston County scene quickly, and using the full resources of his press relations office.

Once bodies started being recovered, and murder warrants sought, Webster's office became aggressive in a manner that started to concern Doug Roberts.

Roberts had the warrants ready to issue once identification was secured on the first three bodies, warrants that would charge both Copelands with first degree murder, punishable by the death penalty.

But, he was told by a member of the Attorney General's staff to hold off on filing the murder charges, to wait until the Attorney General himself could be present in Chillicothe to make the announcement. His schedule was filled for a couple of days, and Roberts wondered out loud about the propriety of delaying filing murder charges so a press conference could be arranged.

"I was told that when you get the help from the AG (Attorney General) then you give a little help back, too," Roberts said later, still shaking his head.

The filing of the murder charges was indeed delayed until Attorney General Bill Webster came to town.

In the initial press release on November 13, 1989, Webster's office touted the Webster press conference slated for Chillicothe, and said, "It is the policy of the Attorney General's office to seek the death penalty." Webster was also quoted as saying that "I've instructed the attorneys and investigators from my office to continue the white collar investigation in this case to determine if probable cause exists to file additional fraud charges for violations of the state's Merchandising Practices Act," an action never taken in this case.

Webster took the unusual step of flying to Chillicothe and holding a press conference in the courthouse to announce the filing of charges. A casual observer may have thought that the state's Attorney General literally typed and delivered the filed charges to the circuit clerk's office. The local officials flanked Webster in the press conference lineup, but added little to what Webster announced that day. Several officials in the photographs from the event have bemused expressions, indicating they know they are part of a relatively strange scene.

Webster, who had made no secret of his desire to run for governor in 1992, issued the second release on December 28, headlined: "Webster, Roberts file five-count indictment in Livingston County against Copelands." The release said, in part, that "Attorney General William L. Webster and Livingston County Prosecuting Attorney Doug Roberts filed . . . ," which hardly deferred to the local prosecutor. The release further quoted Webster: "In multiple murder cases, it is the policy of the Attorney General's office to seek the death penalty. We will do so in this case." The Attorney General's office, by itself, cannot file murder or death penalty charges under state law.

Doug Roberts had only picked up the first hints of the political and judicial power struggle yet to come.

Chapter Ten

Sheriff Leland O'Dell, in his now-frequent trips back and forth from the sheriff's office in downtown Chillicothe to the Copeland farm out past Mooresville (a round-trip of some twenty miles) knew this whole unfolding Copeland case was backwards.

"Usually, you have a body and you look for a murderer," he said to himself and to others more than once in those hectic days that all seemed to fuse into one. "This time, we got a murderer—and just I know we do—but we got no bodies."

The wiry sheriff, gray hair beginning to win out over dark as he aged, was confident and scared, all at the same time. He felt like he and his men, with appropriate help from Missouri State Highway Patrol officers and the Northwest Missouri Major Case Squad, could solve this puzzle. At the same time, he was frightened to think what would happen if they didn't. In his years as sheriff, he'd never once handled a case anything like this one. While parts of the whole scene were exhilarating, even exciting, he also was enough of a political realist to know it was fraught with danger, embarrassment, and political exile.

As the digging and the searching dragged on — and the long spell of warm weather had come to a screeching halt and winter's north winds had roared in a little early — O'Dell got more and more information to go with the seven sacks of evidence he and the other officers had collected at the Copeland house. The evidence from the home, all closely guarded and examined over and over again by the Major Case Squad, included racks of men's clothing, shoes and boots, crudely rendered records, including the mysterious list of names taken from the Polaroid camera case, the two weapons and some ammunition.

Some officers on the Major Case Squad were examining clothing labels and identification tags; others were searching out handwriting specialists, so they could later seek to prove the list was written by one of the Copelands. Other officers were continuing to gather information about the missing men and pull together records from the cattle sale barns and area banks about the fraudulent buying scheme.

But, despite peaking suspicions that drove

investigators to keep looking, the evidence itself did nothing to make a murder case: There were still no bodies.

Prosecuting Attorney Doug Roberts, despite a long and trusting relationship with Deputy Gary Calvert, privately began to wonder if the quiet deputy had overstated the case, if he'd let his imagination run a little wild this time.

Jack McCormick, the guy who had made the Nebraska call, had been captured in Salem, Oregon, and he had a checkbook from the Brookfield bank with him and he was talking to anyone who would listen. None of the sheriff's investigators had ever heard of or seen Jack McCormick, and privately they wondered what he really knew about the Copeland case. A crucial part of his story simply wasn't panning out: They were becoming increasingly sure that no bodies were going to be found on the Copeland farm. Jack McCormick was sticking with the bodies story, but as time dragged on he began to back away from that portion of his tale.

But the intense publicity surrounding the massive search at the Copeland farm was generating call after call to the Major Case Squad center that had virtually taken over the Livingston County jail building.

Telephone callers were telling of places (many of them isolated, forsaken farms) where

Ray Copeland had worked, places he'd had access to in the relaxed farm honor system where workers and gawkers can come and go from land and farm buildings if they are known in the area. Ray Copeland had usually been available over the years for part-time jobs, painting outbuildings, filling old abandoned wells, cleaning fence rows, burning brush and trash. Callers were giving deputies a long list of more sites to investigate now that it appeared the search of the Copeland place was going to be a bust.

There was even a bit of a lynch mob attitude growing in some segments of the community, with callers saying how they never liked the old man Copeland anyway, and how they always figured he was up to no good. Those snubbed, hoodwinked or bilked by Ray Copeland over the years were starting to come out of the woodwork.

The Copeland sons were catching the brunt of the community's anger, with even Wayne and Al's families snubbed and criticized. The sons made a convenient target for the anger emerging about the viciousness of the crimes allegedly committed by their parents. The sons maintained ignorance of the bad check setup and the subsequent killings.

Jack McCormick had already related the all-too-familiar setup: The post office box for an address, the checking account, the practice sale runs and cattle buying, his suspicions about how Ray Copeland was prepared to shoot him in the back of the head.

Gary Calvert was secretly startled at the coarseness, the crudeness, of the Copeland plan. He was also pleased that he had more or less put together the picture before McCormick and the gathering evidence and phone calls were all in place.

Lawmen also made Jack a deal he couldn't refuse: The bad check charges, strung from Missouri to Oregon, would be dropped, overlooked if you will, if he would cooperate in the prosecution of Ray and Faye Copeland, testifying at their trial, helping officers, and staying out of trouble in the meantime.

McCormick's rendition of what he thought was going to happen also gave officers their excuse to file conspiracy charges against the Copeland couple and get them in jail—and apart—where maybe one or both of them would be more willing to talk. It also was enough to finally secure the search warrant.

Jack McCormick knew that his deal with the authorities hinged on those lawmen finding bodies, and linking them to Ray Copeland. He was no novice around the courts and lawmen, and knew the proper "order" of things in the justice system. Without bodies,

Ray Copeland would at best face only another bad check charge, or maybe a conspiracy charge, and McCormick might well see his hoped-for deal for freedom fall apart. Jack followed the area newspapers closely and listened to hourly radio reports from local radio stations covering the unfolding Copeland investigation. He waited and hoped that the massive search in Livingston County would soon yield bodies.

He didn't wait long.

On October 17, 1989, deputies Kurt Reith and Paul Stegmaier punched to success inside the Neil Bryan barn, finally finding three bodies stashed in twelve-inch-deep graves. While the bodies bore no identification, investigators were certain these were some of the men who'd worked for Ray Copeland.

Prosecutor Doug Roberts and coroner Scott Lindley jumped into action after the initial body recovery.

They had the names of those who'd passed the bad checks, and had secured at least tentative background information on where the men were from and if there were any family members around. Once they had the bodies, they secured dental records and other information from those survivors, and were able to finally piece together the identifications.

On Nov. 2, 1989, Lindley issued the following terse statement:

Last evening, November 1, 1989, I released to the North Central Missouri Major Case Squad the identification of the human remains that were found on the Neil Bryan farm at RR 1, Ludlow, Missouri, on October 17, 1989. They are:

A. Paul Jason Cowart of Dardanelle, Arkansas

B. John W. Freeman of Tulsa, Oklahoma

C. Jimmie Dale Harvey of Springfield, Missouri

The human remains that were found at RR Ludlow on the Joe Adams farm on October 25, 1989 has been tentatively identified and I am waiting for further information for positive identification.

Notification of the relatives of Mr. Cowart, Mr. Harvey and Mr. Freeman was done on Wednesday, November 1, 1989.

There are many individuals and organizations that were instrumental in this investigation and in aiding in the identification of these men and they need to be acknowledged at this time:

North Central Missouri Major Case

Squad

Sheriff Leland O'Dell and the Livingston County sheriff's office

Chief of Police Tom Black and the Chillicothe Police Department

Doug Roberts and the Livingston County Prosecutor's Office

Missouri State Highway Patrol

Dr. Jon Rose, MD and the Hedrick Medical Center Lab, X-ray department and staff

Dr. Jim Bridgens, MD, Kansas City, Missouri

Dr. Sam Stout and the University of Missouri Department of Anthropology

Dr. Roger Gier, DMD, MSD, and the University of Missouri at Kansas City School of Dentistry

Boone County Medical Examiner's office, Columbia, Missouri

Lindley Funeral Home Staff

Livingston County Road and Bridge Crew

Minnis Cemetery Service

Lawrence Hinnen and Sons

Missouri Public Service

McDonalds of Chillicothe

Breadeaux Pizza of Chillicothe

HyVee Food Store of Chillicothe

Mrs. Sam Stanmier

The people of Livingston County for their cooperation and support.

The rambling thank yous included medical examiners, hospitals, food stores that catered to the hungry cops, and most of the law agencies involved. Absent was any reference to the Missouri Attorney General's office.

Doug Roberts had signed many an arrest warrant and complaint in his years as prosecuting attorney, an action usually taken routinely and with little afterthought. But on this day, November 13, 1989, he took a deep breath and signed the second set of complaints against the Copelands with relish, setting the stage for the legal wrangles to come:

STATE OF MISSOURI, Plaintiff
vs.
RAY COPELAND, Defendant
COMPLAINT
COUNT 1
The Prosecuting Attorney of the County of Livingston, State of Missouri, charges that the defendant, either acting alone, or knowingly in concert with another, in violation of Section 565.020.1 RSMo., committed the class A felony of murder in the first degree, punishable

upon conviction under Section 565.020.02 RSMo., in that on or about the 1st day of May, 1989, in the County of Livingston, State of Missouri, the defendant after deliberation, knowingly caused the death of Paul J. Cowart by shooting him.

Similar counts were prepared listing December 8, 1988, for the death of John W. Freeman; and October 25, 1988, for the shooting death of Jimmie D. Harvey.

Later, after two more bodies were found, additional charges were added.

The charges were prepared separately, but with the same wording, against Faye Copeland.

The chilling addition to the first degree murder charges against both Ray and Faye Copeland came the same day:

NOTICE OF INTENT TO SEEK THE DEATH PENALTY

Comes now the State of Missouri, through counsel, pursuant to Section 565.005, RSMo., giving notice to Defendant Ray Copeland (and to Faye Copeland) that the state intends to seek the death penalty as to each Count. The State intends to rely on the following aggravating circumstances as to each count

172

herein.

1. The offender committed the offense of murder in the first degree for himself or another, for the purpose of receiving money or any other thing of monetary value from the victim of the murder or another; and

2. The murdered individual was a witness or potential witness in a past or pending investigation or past or pending prosecution, and was killed as a result of his status as a witness or potential witness."

At about this time, Ray Copeland was running his spiel with Leland O'Dell and Gary Calvert, who took turns interviewing him in the videotape room in the jail building. He could be positively talkative on some of the visits, even if he really didn't say much.

While professing no knowledge of the missing workers or the bad checks, Copeland began to come up with a variety of stories, some quite elaborate in their design and detail.

At one point, he detailed seeing "Jack McCormick and a couple of colored guys" involved in dumping a body in a well, and tried more than once to lay the blame on McCormick, who he described as a guy who'd been around the Chillicothe area for years, running a variety of scams.

As the search continued wider and farther from the Copeland farm, Copeland's stories became more bizarre and detailed, but he still professed to have no knowledge of the bodies or any crimes.

"You'll find nothing on my place, let's just say that for sure," Ray told deputies more than once, knowing, of course, that was true.

Once in a while, he would ramble off into other stories, stories about Russian or European cattle buyers and syndicates that bought cattle and the like.

A week after the initial discovery of bodies, searchers went back to the Joe Adams barn they'd already quickly searched once, and decided to dig deeper.

Pulling together more than a dozen deputies and volunteers, several hours were spent removing two thousand bales of hay from one end of the barn, bales stacked ceiling high atop wooden planks.

Under those planks the grisly discovery was revealed: a body, again wrapped in black plastic, again with a single small caliber hole in the back of the head.

The corpse was later identified as Wayne

Warner.

The search continued to grow, and some officers were startled to continue to discover how far Ray Copeland roamed over the Midwest in search of both workers and cattle sales.

About two weeks after Warner's body was discovered, the search reached far south into Benton County, about one hundred and thirty miles from Chillicothe. Reports had surfaced that Ray had attended cattle sales in that region, and had been seen with hired hands on more than one occasion. Nothing was ever found there after a two-day ground search.

There were starting to be calls now from other states, from police with unsolved missing person reports, or agencies with large bad checks and no solution.

Perhaps the saddest calls, however, came from mothers and wives scattered around the nation, women seeking missing men. "I never would have guessed there were that many people missing, that many people just gone," Deputy Gary Calvert said one day.

The detailed records being kept by the Major Case Squad included all the spots that had been searched, and it was a growing stack of paper. The searchers had peered down wells, scoured through old barns, outbuildings and sheds. They'd dug in ditch banks and cattle pen areas and had brought in dog teams from the Kansas State Prison in Lansing, Kansas, dogs trained to sniff out fleeing convicts.

Maybe it was time to retrace the search, to go back over some of the areas with a finer tooth comb. Many of the callers had established one pattern: Ray Copeland had worked around a lot of wells, repairing some, filling and capping others.

An old well about one hundred fifty yards from the Joe Adams barn, where Wayne Warner's body was found, was one of those to be rechecked. The water level had been high in the forty-foot-deep well when it was first checked in mid-October, and now it was down considerably.

The deputies rigged up a grappling hook, and dropped it in the black water, over and over, before finally snagging something other than trash or brush.

They pulled up a cowboy boot, with a foot still in it.

"Jesus," an officer quietly muttered as the boot and foot plopped out on the frozen ground.

Sheriff O'Dell and the officers quickly decided that to lower someone into the well to retrieve the body would be too risky. They would have to dig down beside it, and bust through the lower side of the well before they could recover the rotting remains.

Backhoes were brought in, and most of the water was pumped out of the well. A piece of plywood on a tractor tire inner tube was lowered down to cover the decayed body, in case the walls of the well would collapse before searchers could retrieve the body.

It took nearly a full day to recover the body of Dennis Murphy. A belt buckle with "Dennis" etched into it came out with the body when it was finally hauled out onto a sheet of protective plastic.

Ray Copeland, apparently unaware that Murphy's body had been recovered, was questioned by Sheriff O'Dell that same day, and the specific well on the Adams's farm was mentioned.

Ray Copeland came up with a story ("I tell you this is right") of seeing Jack McCormick, a "colored guy," and maybe a woman, dumping a body down the well. "You might oughta look there," he said, leaning forward to talk to the sheriff, who was busily making notes of the conversation. O'Dell knew, of course, that the body had already been recovered.

"There's a concrete block and a chain around him," Ray Copeland said.

"You say there's a concrete block and a

chain, around his waist, to, uh, weight him down or what," Leland O'Dell asked.

"Yeah, to hold him down."

He was right on that count.

Thomas Buell had fired thousands of weapons in his two decades as a ballistics expert for the Missouri State Highway Patrol.

But he'd not dealt with many firearms like the old rifle taken from the home of Ray and Faye Copeland.

At least three decades old, the Marlin brand bolt-action rifle was a relic of another age: It was beat-up, had spots of rust, and had obviously been well-used over the years.

Along with the rifle and a pistol, Buell had little vials that contained twisted .22 caliber slugs found in the skulls of three of the bodies found in the Copeland search.

His first step was to make sure, to his own satisfaction, that the old rifle was safe to fire. He then used a number of different size .22 caliber bullets available at the Patrol's crime laboratory in the capital city of Jefferson City.

The rifle would be fired, one shot at a time, into a barrel of water and then the slugs retrieved.

With those slugs he'd just fired in hand, Buell then placed them alongside the slugs recovered from the bodies, and placed them under a special scope that allows the slugs to be compared.

Years of criminal ballistics investigation has shown that no two rifles leave exactly the same pattern on slugs fired down their barrel. Unlike shotguns with smooth barrels, rifles have spiraled "rifles" or grooves carved into the inside of every barrel, a technique to spin the bullet on its exit to improve accuracy.

The "rifles" in the barrel whittle away at the slug, leaving unique patterns in the soft metal used in bullets.

If the slug Buell fired from the old Marlin matched those found in the corpses, then the Copeland rifle could be proven to have been the murder weapon.

Buell has run through this science in countless trials over the years, his dry monotone delivery usually convincing juries that he knows what he's speaking about.

Buell matched up the slugs and peered intently into the microscope-like affair that compares the slugs. He adjusted the bullets forward and back, until a line matched.

The slugs in the skulls and the slugs test-fired from the Ray Copeland rifle were a perfect match.

While there was no registration ever proving that Copeland had bought that rifle sometime prior to 1953 (according to Marlin Company serial number records), there was no doubt it came from the Copeland home, and there were a number of witnesses who could testify that the gun was owned by Copeland. Farmers recognize weapons like pickup trucks, and there were many who could testify they'd seen Ray Copeland and the old rifle together.

Jack McCormick would certainly testify to that fact, and still seemed to shudder when he recalled the day he claims Ray Copeland aimed the rifle at him two or three times, but never pulled the trigger.

Thomas Buell's work, in the quiet and near-sterile laboratory, may have helped nail the case against Ray Copeland. Most jurors these days quickly understand and accept ballistics information, and the simplest and possibly most effective point of the prosecution's case would be: This is Ray Copeland's gun, and it fired the shots that killed these men.

No one ever accused David Miller of being flashy or greedy for the printer's ink or the television screen.

A public defender covering the Livingston County area, David Miller had been named to defend Faye and Ray Copeland after they were initially arrested on the conspiracy charges.

A public defender full-time for only a short while when the Copeland case broke, Miller combined an engaging sense of humor with a low-key courtroom style that usually played well in the cases he saw come to trial. Unlike many of the tight-jawed young and eager public defenders so often on cases like this one, David Miller knew his territory; he knew his limits; he knew the brutal facts of the case. He knew that keeping the pair off death row was a realistic goal.

Once describing the efforts by prosecutors to offer Faye Copeland a deal before her trial, Miller said, "They were playing cat and mouse . . . and we didn't have a cat or a mouse or a window to throw either out of."

His small second-floor office, high up at the end of a narrow flight of stairs, is directly across the street from the Livingston County courthouse, and he's called repeatedly to defend clients unable to hire a private attorney.

His initial meeting with Ray Copeland was marked by the old farmer's defiance and near-bragging about his troubles.

"They don't know what they're talking about, they don't know what they're doing," Ray would repeat to Miller. He also denied killing "anyone" when Miller brought up that legal prospect. Ray Copeland appeared almost cocky about his feelings that he was smarter than the lawmen pursuing him.

Faye Copeland, however, was a different person to David Miller. Confused, distraught, and only once in awhile angry, Faye professed no knowledge of what officers were talking about, and never once spoke badly of her husband of nearly fifty years. She appeared to be totally loyal to old Ray, and continued to profess no knowledge of anything illegal.

Miller found himself on a spot. He was faced, on the one hand, with a defiant, gnarled, old farmer who said, "They don't know what they're talking about," and, on the other hand, his longtime wife who professed that she "didn't know what they're talking about."

Faye Copeland's anger, when it surfaced, was toward the prosecutors and lawmen and the turn of events. Miller, however, said he occasionally picked up hints from her that she wasn't happy with her husband's lack of apparent concern for her. She wouldn't admit it in so many words, but she appeared hurt that her husband wasn't in touch with her, trying to check on her, or see to her health and mental state.

The cases were soon split up, after Doug Roberts hinted a deal might be in the offing for Faye Copeland. David Miller felt the case against the grandmotherly lady was less solid than the one building against her husband.

"I doubted a jury was going to convict Faye Copeland, much less sentence her to death," Miller said months later, reflecting an opinion held by most others watching the cases unfold.

The public defenders also had questions and concerns about the involvement of Attorney General Webster in the snowballing case. They issued a statement following Webster's high-profile press conference in Chillicothe:

Barbara Schenkenberg and I, as attorneys for Ray and Faye Copeland, wish to make the following statement:

It has always been our policy to try any case in the Courtroom and not in the Press. This is especially true where our clients are 75 and 68 years of age and have lived in this community for over 25 years.

Unfortunately, since the Attorney General's Office has become involved in this matter, they have insisted upon making this case a media event or even a media circus.

We both feel strongly that Ray and Faye's rights are being severely compromised by the daily flood of baseless innuendo, particularly in light of their frail health.

Earlier today we challenged the Attorney General to take this case into the Courtroom where it belongs, but, unfortunately, it appears they have chosen to continue trial by press release and news conference.

We again challenge them to move this matter out of the media and into the Courtroom where it properly belongs.

(Signed)
David H. Miller
District Defender

Faye had seen Ray in jail, she'd talked with him in the dreary waiting rooms of prisons; she'd smelled those jail smells of cigarettes, body odor, urine, and disinfectant.

But she'd never spent a night in a cell until October 9, 1989.

And now she was fading fast, obviously distraught at being locked up. During her first few days in confinement, she ate almost nothing, and suffered a severe weight loss before doctors were able to nurse her back to a reasonable measure of good health. Her once permed frizzy hair was now just slicked back man-style. Her eyes were sunken and red, and she was weeping, quietly sobbing, most of the time.

But, she'd bounce back some days, seemingly in a better mood, sometimes after brief visits from her sons, sometimes as if she just made up her mind to feel better.

And, she did take a few moments to write a letter to her husband:

hi Ray Honey
Just a few lines to talk a few minutes.
Nothen [sic] found and nothen [sic] gained. . . .
Odell said everything was ng. [sic] as of now. Doug [Roberts] is going to learn one thing for sure. Never no Servis [sic] from me. Should have had Cowder on the Bank Deal.
Digger is gone thay [sic] only had 10 days on warrant it is up Wed. then things will cool down.

After relating a few more facts about the timing of the trial, she signed the letter "Love Mom." The prosecutors entered this letter into evidence later to convince the jurors that Faye was more than an innocent bystander. And, despite her hopes, things never did "cool down."

Chapter Eleven

One of the signs on the wall at Brewer's Barber Shop says it all:

Just What Part of
NO
Didn't You Understand?

There's not much nonsense at the cramped barbershop, located on Jackson Street, a block from the Livingston County courthouse. In this establishment, maybe a last male bastion, haircuts are not a fashion statement, they're merely to shorten the hair. Country and bluegrass music is the only kind of music appreciated or allowed, and justice is meted out in no-nonsense doses of simple right and wrong.

In this shop, Faye and Ray Copeland were people who'd brought shame to the small farming community. He was seen as a tough, mean, old man who'd killed for profit and greed. She was seen as his willing accomplice. The men

187

who frequented this shop, playing Pitch or cribbage, talking country music or succumbing to a shave since their hands or eyes had grown weak, saw their verdict on the Copelands as no colder than what the couple had done to the drifters who became farmhands.

Every Wednesday night, a clutch of mainly old men gather in this small crowded barbershop to pick guitars, pluck banjos, or saw on comfortable old fiddles. There's no pretense about the gatherings, no rules (other than no booze), and few subtleties in the conversation that creeps in between musical numbers. The three-hour gatherings are spread by word of mouth, and all Jack Brewer does is unlock the barbershop and the players amble in. Metal folding chairs are circled around the old barber chair, its KOKEN logo on the footrest worn smooth by years of shoe and boot soles, and the playing begins.

In near-missionary fashion, Jack Brewer and the men and a few women who gather here weekly believe that if the bluegrass and country music they know isn't passed along by playing, it will surely die, and be replaced by "electric-whatzit" music. None of those who gather "read" music, and few have had any formal musical or instrument training, other than decades of listening and picking out the twangs and tastes of the songs.

In between "Black Hawk" or "Kentucky

Moon Waltz," the verdict on Ray and Faye Copeland was certain, and the barbershop justice would be swift. The men had little truck for the legal niceties, or with the lawyers earning new three-piece suits on the case, or bothersome things like rules of evidence or even constitutional rights. They were concerned about justice and about the health of the county's budget for trials and jail.

To most who gathered here for the Tuesday through Saturday daytime card games and chatter, the Copeland murder case was very simple: The gun found in Ray Copeland's house fired the slugs that went into the back of the victims' heads, and that was more than enough. *Period*.

"The old fart should be nailed to the wall," Jack Brewer would say, grimacing as he thought of Ray Copeland. "Her, too, by God, she knew what was going on out there, she knew all about it." These men, at least in front of one another, weren't about to buy the "dominated woman theory." They were married, after all, and had little doubt in their own minds about who actually ran things at their homes.

They really didn't know Copeland all that well, only in passing, but they knew all they needed to know about the case, thanks to the daily reports and ultra-black headlines from the local *Constitutional-Tribune* and the nightly bleatings from the Kansas City television stations.

Down and across the street a half-block, at Pam's Cafe, the mood was equally harsh most of the time. Ray Copeland had stopped in the small cafe several times over the years, for a cup of coffee and a piece of pie. He even stopped by there in the late summer some years to sell cantaloupes he'd raised on his farm. But the mood at the small cafe (six booths, five tables, and eight counter stools) was not to forgive or forget what cops said he'd done out at his little farm. Even next door, at the pricier Harlow's, where reporters on expense accounts and lawyers on the public dole dined, there seemed to be little doubt about the guilt of the Copelands.

Pam's owner Joan Anderson, while having little trouble buying what officers said about Ray Copeland, did keep a few doubts about the depth of involvement by Faye. "Just don't know," she'd say, wiping down a just vacated countertop. "Sure seems to me like she had a tough life with him, and maybe she didn't know nothing 'bout what he did . . . just don't know."

Out at the tiny settlement of Mooresville, and near to the Copeland farm, the reaction was predictable, and equally firm: Ray Copeland was absolutely guilty, and opinion was rapidly coming around to Faye's guilt. There was also a sense in the air that most here simply wanted the case to go away: That if old Ray died in his sleep one night, old age finally catching him, that'd be just fine, thank you.

Copeland neighbor Bonnie Thompson, who would later be one of the string of witnesses at the couple's separate trials, had little time for either Copeland and made no secret of it.

She lived close enough to the Copeland farm that she could see the place through her binoculars, and she did just that on more than one occasion. Rural residents tend to become conscious of their "neighborhoods" and are wary of strangers and events that appear out of the ordinary, though few publicly go to the extremes of Bonnie Thompson.

Thompson's concern was that Ray Copeland was bringing drunks and winos into the community, a move she would have piously resisted. As for Faye, Bonnie said, "She was just as mean as he was. She would take the Lord's name with every other word . . . she could be one mean sister, that's for sure. She's as guilty as he is."

Thompson, a not-so-friendly neighbor of the Copelands for sixteen years, said she'd heard Ray brag about his wife. "He used to say she was a good shot, a bull's-eye . . . thinking about that now gives me the creeps."

One of the theories making the rounds, dealing with Faye's involvement, depended upon belief in the Jack McCormick stories. If old Jack could be believed, then Ray aimed that rifle at him at least a couple of times and couldn't pull the trigger, he chickened out. Maybe Faye was the shooter, or so some theories claimed.

Harshness, even violence per se, is not unknown in these rural farming areas, where virtually everyone has guns for hunting and plinking tin cans on a Sunday afternoon. But violence toward deer or stray animals or even "air shots" to frighten off thieves or vandals is one thing; executing men who trusted you, who saw you as their last solid hope of straightening out their twisted lives . . . well, that was clearly another thing. Most families, too, have a "wanderer" in their ranks, a black sheep perhaps; the thought of someone wasting a guy simply because he was vulnerable rubbed most the wrong way.

In nearby Ludlow, such as it is, grocery owner Martha Henderson, a favorite lately of the swarming television camera crews, fretted about the county's expenses for the upcoming trials, and bristled at reports that the county was paying medical expenses in the thousands of dollars for the jailed Copelands.

Henderson had a theory about Ray Copeland's alleged health problems: "Maybe if he hadn't been doing all that digging, he wouldn't have back problems," she said, the stab of humor barely disguising her disgust at the turn of events.

The "Diggin' Up Bones" theme of the search and subsequent arrests and murder charges were borne out in black humor and crude references to the Copelands and their deeds. Some jokes that made the rounds came in several versions, but basically went something like this:

"Did you hear about the new book coming out on the Copelands?"
"No."
"Well, it's going to be called *How to Make a Killing on 40 Acres.*"

Ray Copeland goes into a pickup dealership and expresses interest in a new truck.
The dealer says, "Sure, Ray, but it'll cost you an arm and a leg."
"No problem," Ray says. "Be back in a minute or two."

Generally, despite occasionally laughing at public mistakes or overstatement, people usually want to believe their lawmen. Leland O'Dell dropped off candidate cards by the cash register at places likes Pam's and the Ludlow Market every four years, and everyone knew him and most voted for him. While they might snicker about his struttings from time to time, they knew that when the chips were down, they were going to back the law.

Around the courthouse square and in homes across Chillicothe and Livingston County, little else but the Copeland case was being talked about these days.

Perhaps the only debate was some misgiving, sparked by the Copeland children as much as anything else, as to the guilt, or degree of guilt, of Faye Copeland.

At the Holiday Hotel, where Faye had worked for several years, owner Neeta Patel was flabbergasted and couldn't believe Faye had anything to do with the killings. The Copeland children who lived nearby, Al and Wayne and their wives and children, had come to terms with Ray's guilt, but not with Faye's involvement.

The reigning argument against Faye's involvement was that Ray Copeland had called all the shots (no pun intended), and that his wife of nearly fifty years was kept in the dark on almost everything that happened.

That argument held few backers at Brewer's Barber Shop.

"They were just flat-dab mean, that's all," said one customer. "Just mean, and, hell, they got caught. String 'em up, that's what."

Chapter Twelve

Livingston County had been in existence for more than seven decades before the good citizens finally agreed where to put an appropriately majestic courthouse. After Chillicothe (likely named by early settlers who'd passed through Chillicothe, Ohio) was mapped out in 1837, and then picked as the county seat of government two years later, none-too-fancy courthouses stood at a couple of sites, just outside the bustling little farm town.

In 1913, voters mustered up enough "Yes" votes for a $100,000 bond issue to build a fitting monument on the site of the Elm Street Park, smack in the center of town. Local building designer Warren Roberts was hired to sketch out the striking, classical-design building. The construction was under way at about the same time a massive, new, state, domed capitol building was being erected two hundred miles away in Jefferson City, and the marble in much of the structure was cut from quarries in Bedford, Indiana.

The farmers, merchants, and preachers, who controlled rural Missouri counties as the state developed, wanted fitting monuments to county government, built in part on their firmly held belief that the county governmental organization was the ideal form of government, democracy at its best. Elaborate, ornate, sometimes garish courthouses can be found in many of the state's 114 counties, many now unable to maintain and operate the expensive, impractical structures as farm and town populations have declined and the tax base has continually eroded.

But today's economic realities were not on anyone's mind when the cornerstone for the Chillicothe and Livingston County structure was laid in 1913 and when the building proudly opened for county business the next summer. Two-foot-thick walls, wide, handsome marble stairways, and an open-dome area up through the middle of the building gave it a feeling of permanence and solidity that befit the local residents' pride in their home-based government.

In the decades following, however, with ever-changing governments and economic concerns, the Livingston County courthouse fell into familiar contempt. Layers of paint eventually covered handsome oak woodwork around doorways and on interior walls. Massive, beautiful rolltop desks were later stashed in the drafty, dusty attic, alongside classic glass-front oak bookcases and wide-seated wooden chairs. Huge chandeliers that spread glorious baths of light across the third-floor courtroom and open stairways were removed in favor of more modern fluorescent tubes and starkly modern light fixtures.

When Charlene Coleman first ran for the County Commission in 1984, she made no secret of her love of antiques and restoration work. She said she hoped to return the courthouse to its former internal and external glory. Voters apparently were just as concerned about the declining stature of the courthouse and approved of her grand plans for the structure. Coleman, an energetic, hardworking, onetime schoolteacher, was elected. She went to work on the massive project, literally helping strip layers of paint off oak stair railings and around door facings in her first months of office. She later got more bogged down in the paperwork of county government and reluctantly hired part-time help for the project. Later, working with the judges and prosecutors, she directed county prisoners as they worked off jail sentence time stripping paint, polishing marble, and cleaning windows. Some inmates grumbled about the hard work, most finally decided it beat sitting around in a smelly cell all day. Some of the inmates actually became enthused about the project, working out frustrations with sandpaper rather than whiskey. Striking dark green and black and white inlaid tile floors, in elaborate patterns, colors and designs, were shined back to their original glory. The courthouse was coming back to its initial shine and polish.

She managed to recover and restore the handsome light fixtures that hung over the sweeping stairways, but she never has found the handsome chandeliers that hung above the courtroom. They were removed years ago, and likely ended up gathering dust in an antique store somewhere, the commissioner figures. "I'd sure like to find them, though," she says, wincing at the modern light fixtures, appliances that might brighten up an Army barracks, but which add little to the handsome courtroom.

Some of the other alterations to the handsome building couldn't be easily fixed, either. In the early 1960s, just on the eve of the fateful arrival of edge-of-town shopping malls and fast-food restaurants, downtown merchants and the city government talked the county out of some of its ground around the courthouse for more metered parking, a sore point yet with many, including Charlene Coleman.

Downtown merchants, fighting to hang on, were convinced that more parking would equal more shoppers, a kind of new math that eventually didn't compute. But, the decision chopped up the relatively modest grounds around the courthouse, changes that likely will never be restored.

Other changes and improvements in the striking old building are yet to be made.

"And, the clocks don't work," she'll tell visitors, pointing to the four huge motionless clocks at the tops of the walls, sitting out in front of an only slightly pointed red tiled roof. The clocks stopped running years ago, at various points on their respective dials, and estimates say it would be at least ten thousand dollars to fix them back to running shape and keep them that way for a few years. That's money the county simply doesn't have.

But, while the work continues, the Livingston County courthouse has become one of the most handsome in Missouri, especially once visitors are inside the building. In normal times the courthouse serves the needs of the county of about fifteen thousand folks more than adequately. Taxes and traffic fines are grudgingly paid, taxes are levied and property values assessed, and the building serves as home to the local county agent and assorted record-keepers. It's a gathering place for the old men who spin yarns and spit tobacco, and warm spring evenings will find many of the town's young people leaning against their cars around the square.

The wide marble stairs have smooth, worn indentations from years of shoe and boot soles. A large American flag hangs down in the center of the open-dome area, and wall plaques list not the names of those from Livingston County who died in past wars, but everyone who was ever in the military service. It's an impressive list.

There are also ominous, not-so-polite warning signs posted inside and outside the structure, generally the work of a busy and efficient cleaning staff. Six signs near entry doors warn that there will be "Positively NO LOAFING in courthouse," another pair of signs warns against sitting on the heat registers. A sign above the water fountain gives comfort to those who come to the courthouse thirsty: "Please do not spit Skoal in fountain." Outside signs warn against skateboarding and loitering.

In the years since the city added parking (and the loathsome meters), the economy of the once-bustling square around the courthouse has dramatically changed. The parking meters were unceremoniously yanked out years ago, many of the once-prosperous courthouse square businesses have folded or moved or scaled back their operation, and arts and crafts stores and service companies and lawyers' offices now fill much of the former commercial area.

But the courthouse is still the dominant structure in Chillicothe, the center of the downtown street network and, at least in normal times, simply a place locals can take pride in but otherwise pretty well take for granted.

But the fall of 1990 was not a "normal time" in Chillicothe, a community by now sadly almost used to the horror stories about Ray and Faye Copeland and what had happened out on that Mooresville farm. It had become almost ordinary now to see and hear huge humming television remote broadcast trucks, with satellite dishes erect, parked around the town square, as exotic-appearing camera people talked to a lens. Local kids were figuring out that if they oh-so-casually walked just at the right distance and angle from the camera they could be briefly seen on the evening news. Scruffy newspaper reporters scurried around, often hunched over notepads and coffee in Pam's or the Northside Cafe, or waiting for a pay phone inside the courthouse or at the pair of phones back-to-back on a single post outside. Reporters were forced by the niceties of today's careful news to overuse

201

"alleged" and "charged" while the town generally had dropped any notion of those doubts. And, despite the increasing costs carefully reported by county officials, it was difficult to find locals who resented their tax dollars going to convict the Copeland s. The reporters could also be found comparing notes or quietly making jokes about the Copeland case and fussing about who had the worst editor. The reporter for the local *Constitution-Tribune,* a home-owned daily which still carries garish advertisements high atop the front page, was Ed Crawford, who made a natural combination of tending bar at night and writing stories by day. While he quietly resented the out-of-town reporters working "his" story, he helped most who visited, becoming a regular check for the in-and-out reporters from newspapers and television and radio stations. The cops — local, county, and state — were tight-lipped, especially those from the sheriff's office, and the townspeople were getting to be that way. Sheriff Leland O'Dell had been repeatedly warned by prosecutors, and he heeded those warnings, that untoward or rash comments to reporters would wreck the murder case. He, and his deputies, generally kept mum about the developments in the investigation and trial preparation. Sheriff Greg Coon from nearby Grundy County was the press spokesman for the Major Case Squad and became exceptionally good at the press feedings twice a day: He could say many things about the investigation, in a good-humored and pleasant way, all smiles for the cameras. He had quickly learned how to talk for a relatively long time and really not say anything.

Jim Rice was a hardworking reporter for radio station KMZU who had staked out a spot in front of the sheriff's office for his Ford station wagon, rigged with a homemade and moveable antenna mast. Rice, a hulking, good-natured reporter who could grow more hair these days on his upper lip than on the top of his head, was seldom without a tape recorder, and worked rumors and whispered tips as hard as anyone on the scene. He'd calmly listen to Sheriff Coon's reports, handed out under a couple of potted plants in the lobby of the jail, and then scurry off to track the real rumors and tips he'd heard earlier. When off the air, the triangular tube steel mast splayed down the top of the station wagon, but could be raised quickly when he was on the air. He spent most of the day and night reporting on the search efforts, and had insiders at the sheriff's office keeping him posted on new search sites and reports of bodies. His regular reports became required listening for the visiting reporters. The photographers, both still and television, were perhaps the most frustrated group during the investigation and search, because they could seldom get closer than a few hundred yards from the digging scenes. They were forced to sell editors on press conference pictures or hazy shots from long distances of a clutch of deputies looking in a hole or a dim yellow backhoe digging in a field.

Missouri's rural-dominated legislature, in a move aimed at keeping the costs of trials down for the local counties, had only recently approved a new jury selection system for the state. Under the plan, the jury for a trial would be picked at an out-of-town location, and then brought back to the county where the charges were filed, avoiding costly changes of venue motions that often strapped the "host" county of a major trial, such as the Copeland trials promised to be.

Doug Roberts and Kenny Hulshof had decided early on to split up the trials, to present the cases against Faye and Ray Copeland separately, for a couple of reasons. First, they thought it might be a little harder to convict Faye Copeland , her "grandma" looks perhaps concerning juries. They didn't want potential sympathy for Faye Copeland to sour their case against her husband.

And, perhaps more importantly, they thought if they separated Faye Copeland from the process, she might decide to tell them what really had been going on out at the Copeland place. They were prepared to offer her a greatly reduced charge if she would co-operate.

They figured, wrongly, that Ray Copeland's trial would come first.

Roberts and Hulshof were still getting along fine, and they and two others involved in the case went some two hundred miles south of Chillicothe on a weekend before the trial to plan strategy. Using a cabin at the Lake of the Ozarks resort area that belonged to Doug Roberts's mother-in-law, the four men pored over stacks of documents, divvied up questioning and cross-examination chores, and generally plotted out the strategy of the complicated case. It was a civil, productive time, one that surely helped the trial presentation.

Hoping Faye would talk, however, turned out to be a mistake. She wasn't going to budge. And, she even fought to have her trial first, after it appeared that Ray was going to stay occupied in mental competency hearings. Prosecutors had planned all along to have Ray Copeland's trial first, hoping that the easiest case would break the more difficult one.

Doug Roberts offered Mrs. Copeland a solid deal before her trial began, and she begged off, claiming to have no knowledge of anything that had happened at the Mooresville farm home.

Roberts told her, through her public defender attorney David Miller, and with the knowledge of her sons Al and Wayne Copeland , that he could charge her with conspiracy to commit murder. This meant only several months or a few years in jail, if she would simply tell them where more bodies might be found.

She quickly refused, claiming she didn't know anything about any bodies. Her first degree murder trial, with the added possibility of execution, moved ahead.

"She just wouldn't budge," Roberts recounted later.

Prosecutors felt the case against Faye Copeland basically had two weak spots: First, and frighteningly, Jack McCormick. Would he show up? Would he be sober? Would he throw them a loop in the testimony? Could they count on him to make that all-important connection between Ray Copeland and Faye Copeland ? Secondly, they were concerned about the willingness of a jury to convict an elderly woman. Would they be swayed by her tears? What if she takes the stand and pleads for her life?

The prosecutors weren't that concerned about the evidence. The facts of the case spoke for themselves.

The relatively new out-of-town jury system was used to pick those who would hear the case against Faye Copeland , with key lawyers in the case traveling 160 miles south to Nevada, Missouri, in Vernon County.

The jurors were then bused to Chillicothe, and preparations began for a 3:00 P.M., Monday, November 1, 1990 trial start, in proceedings some predicted could take three weeks. It's not unusual in Missouri's courts for a murder trial to start and end within two days, and talk of a three-week trial startled some longtime court observers.

Kenny Hulshof, with his young Robert Redford good looks and not-so-secret ambition, relished the Copeland case, starting with the jury selection. A relative newcomer on the Attorney General's staff, he regarded getting the high-publicity case a feather in his cap, and he wasn't about to shirk any details, any realistic chance he had to make the case stick.

Perhaps a little too sporty for parts of rural

Missouri, driving his black Porsche to the courthouse each morning, Hulshof, however, soon won over the jury and the spectators. He was dramatic, hard-charging, and more than willing to talk to any reporters who had a question.

Doug Roberts, on the other hand, stayed a little uptight about the growing case. Despite more than a decade as a prosecutor, he'd never handled a case even approaching the magnitude of this one. He had never prosecuted a capital case where execution by lethal injection could well be the result.

Missouri had recently opted for lethal injection execution, scrapping the old gas chamber booth. The lethal injections, conducted in sterile conditions in a new prison in Potosi, Missouri, had been used, and state juries were showing increasing desire to send those convicted of murder to death row. At the time the Copeland s were charged, there were more than fifty on death row, and it was a nearly ten-year wait between conviction and eventual execution.

The argument that it was futile to sentence two persons the age of the Copeland s to death was heard, primarily from editorial writers appropriately remote from the Livingston County horror. But in the coffee shops, down at Brewer's Barber Shop, or out at the HyVee grocery store, most backed "going all the way" against the Copeland s.

Politically, Doug Roberts was getting hammered by the coffee shop crowd almost daily, with urgings that he "nail" the elderly couple. There was little sympathy anywhere around Livingston County for the Copeland s, with most local residents more than willing to see them prosecuted and executed.

Roberts and Hulshof had established a solid working and social relationship, and with the trial date approaching, it was clear they had divvied duties and were intent on pursuing the case against Faye Copeland .

It was a relationship, however, that was going to be strained and finally broken over the next several weeks.

This day, all eyes were on the opening arguments, and the crowded courtroom was anxious to see just what kind of case the state had against Faye Copeland .

There was an assumption that "Old Ray" was guilty as hell, but what about Faye?

Chapter Thirteen

The harried sheriff, Leland O'Dell, wanted nothing to go wrong at this high-profile trial of Faye Copeland. The Copeland case had drawn intense interest, from lawyers, the curious, and the press. Articles about the aged couple had appeared from New York to the West Coast, and he was being hit daily with requests from a variety of persons interested in the case. He never, in all his years as sheriff, had conducted a trial under this kind of spotlight.

Down a flight of stairs from the third-floor courtroom where the trial would take place, the sheriff stepped back, eyeballing the eight-foot-long table that was sitting at an angle just past the landing on the second-floor Livingston County courthouse. This was to be the security checkpoint for the deputies and Missouri State Highway Patrol officers assigned to keep order and screen spectators at the Faye Copeland trial. Officers didn't quite know what to expect at this high-publicity trial, a highly unusual occurrence in this courtroom. Would the relatives of one of the victims try to take out Faye or Ray? Would someone have a grudge against the judge or lawyers? Whatever, they took no chances, and closely screened everyone who came to the courtroom. They never found a weapon, and never really had any problems with the spectators.

The long table, yellow legal pads in place, was where officers planned to sit to take down the names of those attending, after checking identification: names of reporters and television folks on one pad, spectators on another. Green-trimmed, white, sticky name tags would be written out for each person in the courtroom, except the lawyers working the case, who were waved through daily.

Deputies were to operate the handheld metal detectors that would screen those heading for the courtroom. Pocketknives were to be held back in most cases, according to the rules established in a series of meetings before the trial was to get under way. The screenings would take place each morning, after the lunch break, and before any evening sessions.

Long lines formed before each session, as

people waited patiently and then tried to look nonchalant as a deputy ran a metal detector over their bodies.

Sheriff Leland O'Dell and Judge E. Richard Webber, a special judge called from his home courtroom in Memphis, Missouri, also had laid out some other rules: no cameras, no tape recorders. The crowds of spectators and reporters were to be kept completely away from Faye Copeland when she came in or out of the courthouse from jail.

Judge Webber, from a rural judicial circuit north of Chillicothe, was named to hear the case after the local judge was disqualified. A veteran prosecutor and judge for more than a dozen years, Judge Webber knew more than most what to expect in the convoluted and lengthy trial, and helped the local officials prepare for the press and spectators.

Webber, forty-seven at the start of the Faye Copeland trial, was a law graduate of the nearby University of Missouri, and had been a prosecuting attorney in Schuyler, Scotland, and Putnam counties before being appointed to fill an unexpired term in the state's First Judicial Circuit. He had lost his left arm in a farm accident as a teenager, wore an artificial arm and was given to lengthy, solitary walks around Chillicothe during noontime breaks. He seemed to enjoy the jurors and had supper with them one evening, a point criticized by defense lawyers in subsequent appeals. He was intent on moving the trial forward, and had planned for rarely used Saturday sessions long before the proceedings began.

Courtroom proceedings are not televised in Missouri, so the officials rightly anticipated a few sketch artists would be around through the trial, and blocked out front-row seating.

The deputies knew it was going to be a long trial, nothing like the usual one- and two-day trials so common in this courthouse. The coffee pot and a box and sack of doughnuts were not too far away.

The trial would take place in the third-floor courtroom, a handsome, wide-open room with white high ceilings and a number of outside windows. U.S. and state flags banked behind the judge's bench, and the lawyers for prosecution and defense had a long wooden table each. The entryway at the top of the steps was separated from the courtroom by a glass wall, meaning those standing outside taking a break or smoking a cigarette could at least see the proceedings, even if they couldn't hear them. Eight rows of church-style pews arched around the room, potentially meaning three hundred could easily find a place to sit.

Jurors were to sit in a double row of wooden chairs to the spectators' right, and before the trial was over deputies would make a special trip to the nearby Wal-Mart for thick cushions to soften the stern juror chairs.

As Deputies Kurt Reith and Lloyd Macholz and others stewed about the preparations on that first day, Faye Copeland was fretting, too. Chillicothe police woman Renee Brinkley, assigned during most of Faye Copeland's jail time to watch over her, stood silently as Faye repeated her usual morning routine and cleaned and puttered around in her cell. But the busy-work couldn't hide the terror on Faye's face: She had never been in court before, and was nervous and frightened.

She put on a plain white sweater over her black slacks and light blouse, and sat on her cell bed and waited. Leland O'Dell and deputies finally came, trying to be as polite as they could.

"We need to go, Mrs. Copeland," Leland O'Dell said softly.

"Yes," Faye answered quietly.

Outside, the bright sunlight momentarily startled Faye, who had become accustomed to the muted light of the jail cell. She was carefully helped into the backseat of the sheriff's car, and O'Dell drove, with Renee Brinkley in the front seat, the short distance to the parking lot at the west door of the courthouse.

An elbowing crowd of television cameramen and still photographers had already staked out positions around the outside courthouse doorway, hoping for that "opening day shot" that's become mandatory with the evening news or in the morning paper.

Deputies had roped-off a section of the side lot parking area, and were able to pull right up to the courthouse door and hustle Mrs. Copeland to the door. Deputies weren't afraid that the sixty-nine-year-old woman, usually crying or mumbling to herself, was going to make a break for freedom. Rather, they feared that someone—maybe a relative of a victim, maybe a disgruntled local resident with a hunger for publicity—might try to hurt her.

Faye Copeland seemed in a daze when she passed through the bank of cameras, ignoring shouted requests from photographers and reporters for a comment. She was already confused and addled by the proceedings themselves, starting to use an ever-handy tissue to wipe her eyes and nose. It was going to be a long day, one of many, for the frail grandmother.

She was taken to a small side room off the courthouse to wait for the proceedings to begin. Some mornings she huddled there with her attorney, or one or both of her sons.

Jurors, fresh from the three-hour bus ride from Nevada, appeared anxious to get things going. They'd heard bits and pieces of the case during the juror questioning sessions, and had at least a vague idea of what they were getting into. They knew, of course, they were dealing with a case where the eventual penalty could be lethal injection in the state's maximum security prison.

Upstairs in the courtroom, Kenny Hulshof and Doug Roberts huddled together, making sure the evidence they wanted to show the jury was present. They tried to anticipate any comments from David Miller, who tried, more or less in vain, to comfort Faye Copeland. Miller knew he had an uphill battle in front of him. The prosecutors exuded confidence.

Ray Copeland was still in jail, and was away in a state mental hospital for evaluations during a portion of the trial. He had been examined by a number of doctors and psychiatrists. He was apparently oblivious to the peril facing his wife of half a century. He never once asked about her trial or her welfare during the days of testimony, and he could not hear radio or television reports. He simply didn't seem to care.

Judge Webber, after talking briefly with the spectators and telling them in general terms how the courtroom procedures would work and what he expected of them, called for opening arguments.

This was Kenny Hulshof's time to shine. His mother was among those packed into the courtroom.

"The common thread to this case is the human element," Hulshof told the jurors, taking a stand behind a slight lectern facing the jury. "You're going to experience the life of a transient over the next few days. Most of these men had little financial means, but they had hope that tomorrow will bring a brighter day . . . maybe somebody will rescue them.

"You'll also hear from Jack McCormick." (A key player in the state's case against both Faye and Ray Copeland, yet someone prosecutors knew could have his credibility picked apart by defense lawyers. It was important that they paint a warts-and-all portrait of Jack McCormick, at least as far as they could.) "He's been all over the U.S., he was a drifter, and in the fall of 1988 he ended up at Victory Mission in Springfield, Missouri. Jack McCormick was a street alcohol bum, he sold his blood to buy drinks . . ."

Kenny Hulshof continued to walk the jury through Ray Copeland's pitch to Jack McCormick at the mission: the offer of fifty dollars a day, room and board, cattle sales. Then he started to bring Faye Copeland into the scene.

After Ray and Jack arrived at the Copeland home, Hulshof told jurors, "Faye met them, with dinner waiting," and said that McCormick was told of the post office box and bank account setup in front of Faye.

Faye Copeland had her once-curly hair slicked back, up and over her ears. The mixture of dark and graying hair made her scarcely resemble the earlier appearance in pictures taken before the murder charges were filed. Her reddened eyes would one moment peer intently at the witnesses or prosecutor, and then seem to drift away to seemingly other thoughts. She clutched a tissue in her hands, and was almost constantly wiping her eyes or nose. Public Defender

Miller, who earlier tried to comfort her, seemed intent on listening to Hulshof and checking his remarks against what he planned to tell jurors. Two of the Copeland sons, Al and Wayne, were among the spectators, their faces difficult to read as they listened to the case being opened.

". . . Found in a camera case was a list of names, including one she'd earlier denied knowing and Faye Copeland wrote that list," Kenny Hulshof said. "Next to many of those names was an 'X'."

At moments like that in the testimony or comments, Faye would sometimes shake her head in a "no" motion, her eyes sometimes angrily branding the words as lies.

Faye Copeland had expressed intense anger toward Doug Roberts in conversations with David Miller before the trial; her anger apparently aimed at someone she knew. She didn't seem to have the same animosity toward Kenny Hulshof, for example, because she had not known or even seen him before the trial started.

But when Hulshof discussed the list found, noting it was in Faye Copeland's handwriting, at which point Faye vigorously shook her head in a no-no motion again.

David Miller was low-key and plodding with the jury. He laid out what he thought were simple denials.

"There will not be evidence in cattle records of Faye Copeland's participation," David Miller said. "She's not on the bank records."

Referring to the list of names, Miller said, "She was a compulsive list maker . . . maybe it was an effort to organize her thoughts about what had been going on at her house."

Then the public defender launched in to what he saw as the heart of his defense of Faye Copeland.

"This is a picture of a lady married for practically fifty years, a picture of a lady I term trapped, in the worst sense of the word, in an old-fashioned marriage . . . this woman was placed in a situation where she couldn't question the activities of her husband.

"She would be told to mind her own business, to shut her mouth, told she was stupid. Ray's business was Ray's business, and not hers," Miller said calmly to the jurors, intently listening on this comfortable afternoon. Warm outside light beamed into the courtroom through the handsome windows that ringed three walls.

"Faye Copeland may be as much a victim as anyone else," Miller said.

For Al and Wayne Copeland, the pain and anger they'd felt for months came to a head when the trial began. They had been harassed, their children had been teased and accused in school, and they had joined much of the rest of the community in agonizing over what had been going on out at the Copeland place.

Wayne, his anger sometimes spilling over, would huddle with his brother Al outside the courtroom during breaks, staying near the gurgling water fountain or the large ashtrays spotted in the small lobby area outside the courtroom. They seldom spoke to others attending the trial, though they kept at least a nodding acquaintance with the sheriff and some of his deputies as they came and went from the courtroom. Gary Calvert had talked to both Copeland sons extensively through the investigation leading up to the trial. While they had some respect for him, they thought he'd joined with the rest of the lynch mob in lumping their mother in the murder charges.

As the trial opened, both sons seemed convinced that their mother would be cleared of charges, a mood that shifted as the trial wore on.

Al, as best he could, kept a smile and tried to find something ironic or amusing about the family tragedy unfolding in front of his eyes. He still was dismayed that the charges had been brought against his mother, but didn't doubt, sadly, what he'd been discovering about his father.

Wayne, an active sportsman and gun expert, had been involved in a state-sponsored gun safety program for a number of years before the case broke. He was quietly asked to step aside from that task after his parents were arrested.

Not long after the arrest of the elderly Copelands, Al lost his job of seven years, even though that wasn't the official reason, he was told. But, he knew better in his own mind. Perhaps the cruelest reaction came when Al and his wife Brenda found out they could no longer serve as emergency foster parents, after a long and successful stint in that role.

The community was not gentle with the boys, many thinking they may have either helped their father in his evil scheme, or at least received some of the money. Neither thought ever proved even remotely true.

It was a gruesome time for the men, who

desperately wanted the community to know that just because Ray Copeland was their father did not mean they were close or involved in his affairs. The tension that started in a cow milking barn decades earlier in Illinois was still present, and they delved little into their father's day-to-day doings. Even if the boys had truly ever wanted to be close to their father, it's certain he would never have allowed it.

But their father's activities had finally come crashing down on them. While they felt no joy in the problems facing their father, they felt no great shock or sympathy, either.

Their feelings toward their mother, however, were different. Both men felt she was taking a fall for their father, just as she had done all her life. They also knew in their hearts, their mother had always been treated like they were: Ray Copeland was crude, coarse, mean, and threatening with the whole family. And, the sons shook their heads when they repeated their father's contention that he would soon be freed, that the cops weren't smart enough to catch him, that he'd be back out at the farm in a day or two. "He really believes that," Al would say, a wry smile barely covering the pain.

"Mom was never allowed to know what

dad was doing, and that never changed all her life," Al Copeland said one day during one of the pretrial hearings. "She was as scared of him as we were, and he did whatever he pleased. Always did."

For both Copeland sons, the anger toward the press varied from humorous to threatening, and they seldom mixed with others who attended the courtroom proceedings. Mike McCann, a bearded reporter from the *St. Joseph News-Press/Gazette,* was one of only a handful of people to gain the confidence of the Copeland sons, his friendly demeanor and constant efforts to be fair paying off journalistically. McCann spent countless hours and highway miles covering the case for his newspaper, attending obscure pretrial hearings, and becoming a fixture in the mix of people always surrounding either of the Copelands. His newspaper circulates in the Chillicothe area, and the coverage was widely respected by his peers and the subscribers.

The first day ended quickly because of its late start, and some of the crowd was noticeably disappointed that the trial wasn't more exciting. It seemed humdrum and even tedious at times.

Some indicated they weren't coming back,

though at least two of the spectators huddled with the press photographers outside and tried to get a snapshot of Faye Copeland being led to the sheriff's car.

The courtroom never was filled to overflowing. It was as if many in Chillicothe simply wanted their lives to get going again . . . for Ray and Faye Copeland to be out of their lives.

But, the stakes were huge, and both sides were ready for the legal wars to come — crowd or no crowd.

Chapter Fourteen

The little man sort of swaggered down the wide aisle that split the row of pews in the Livingston County courtroom. Wearing a rust-colored, wide-lapelled and misfitted leisure suit, clean shaven and seemingly bright-eyed, Jack McCormick looked like a door-to-door salesman sizing up a neighborhood.

McCormick's turn to take the witness stand came after a rash of lesser witnesses, those who basically were repeating information about the many items taken from the Copeland house and setting up proof that Faye Copeland's "hi, Honey" letter to Ray was sent through jail mail channels, and that it was indeed written by Faye.

Jack McCormick was ready for his day in court, a confident look in his eyes. The sun filtered through the large windows, facing the courthouse square, and bounced and shone off his bald head. He identified himself, and then suddenly, only a few minutes after Kenny Hulshof started questioning him, he butted in.

"You said yesterday I was a bum and I want to correct that. I wasn't a bum. I was a tramp. A bum doesn't work, a tramp does," McCormick said snappily to a stunned and momentarily speechless Hulshof. "I worked to get money to buy drink."

Hulshof recovered his composure, and then had Jack run through the checkered story of his life, at least in a very condensed and somewhat sanitized version. Jack readily admitted he "drank to stay drunk," and that he had spent much of the past few years "just tramping around" and that he had been sending his life "into the gutter."

He talked about the death of his wife in Idaho a decade earlier, a tragedy he implied may have played a role in his eventual downfall. He described his travels from Florida to Alaska, talked about his "blackouts" after too much booze. He briefly mentioned his family, including a son he says lives in Saudi Arabia. He also admitted to earlier convictions on credit card fraud and for various drinking, stealing, and driving offenses.

He said after landing in Springfield, Missouri, he'd tried to straighten his life out, becoming active and even taking a leadership role in the Christian Life Program, helping others who were going down roads he'd already traveled many times.

He then described his initial meeting with Ray Copeland, vividly recalling the old farmer's massive "hook nose," bib overalls and his old pickup truck. He repeats the pitch he says Copeland used on him, a line that eventually convinced Jack to come to work in Chillicothe.

He then begins to weave Faye Copeland into the story, pointing out her interest in the setup of the checking accounts and the fact that she fixed the meals and saw that he was set up in the second bedroom of the Copeland home.

He also said he had observed her doing chores with her husband around the farm, even feeding the pigs sometimes, and that she would ask "if everything went alright" when Jack and Ray came back from the distant cattle and livestock sales. "She also kept all the banking records, the things like that," McCormick said. He spoke with an air of confidence that backed up his reputation as someone who could sell ice cubes to Eskimos. During breaks in questioning, such as during bench conferences with the judge, Jack would turn and look at the jury members, sizing up how he was going over.

He repeats his story about wandering around on the Copeland farm one quiet Sunday afternoon, and being strongly reprimanded by Faye in no uncertain terms.

"She come running out there and says 'Don't you ever go walking around this place,' " Jack McCormick tells the jurors.

Faye then visibly tenses in her wooden chair at the defense lawyer table and mutters, "That's a lie!"

McCormick, who managed to create a few snickers in the tiring crowd through his lengthy testimony and his deadpan accounts of his storied life, then relayed his version of his final hours at the Copeland farm.

He says he saw black plastic on the back of a trailer behind the tractor and heard Ray Copeland call him to help with a "chore" in the barn. He says Ray was carrying his old rifle, and wanted Jack to roust out a 'coon he said was in the barn.

Jack used a stick to poke for the hidden 'coon, and catches a glimpse of Ray Copeland aiming the gun at him. Jack said he then decided "not to take my eyes off him again," and Faye begins crying openly, heard in the courtroom for the first time. She buries her head in her hands.

Jack also describes his demands to leave,

and how he eventually eluded the Copelands and made his way West.

At the end of the opening testimony, Hulshof asked McCormick about his Nebraska telephone call, and Jack looked squarely at the jury and admitted part of what he said was a lie. "I admit to exaggerating (about seeing bodies and bones) but I was trying to get their attention."

The trial bogged down somewhat after the Jack McCormick testimony, perhaps understandably, and during a rare Missouri court Saturday session, the courtroom briefly resembled a Goodwill clothes closet.

Tedious identification work was needed to introduce the pieces of clothing found in the Copeland house, pants and work shirts and shoes that belonged to some of the missing men. In addition, several hours of court time were taken in the piece-by-piece introduction of the bounced checks and examination of bankers and sale barn owners involved in the illegal transactions.

In addition, the forensic testimony was long and involved, as was the testimony tied to the identification of the bodies.

Doug Roberts slept fitfully the night of November 9, the night before he knew he was going to ask the jury he'd been staring at all week to convict a sixty-nine-year-old woman of five counts of murder.

The jurors, who watched the events unfold carefully during seven full days of testimony, still were looking at what could have been anybody's grandmother: This weeping, nearly hysterical, old woman didn't look the part of a serial killer or someone involved in a string of murders covering at least three years.

Roberts knew it was going to be the moment of his law career.

He started softly and carefully with the jury, stating the obvious. "We know the five men who worked on her farm are dead. And each and every one of them had a connection to that woman before they died," he said, turning to point to Faye.

He then walked toward the jury, carrying the .22 caliber rifle that ballistics tests had proven killed the buried men.

"This weapon came out of her home.

"If she didn't know them, what were their clothes doing in her house?

"If she didn't know them, why are their names on this list?

"She lied about not knowing them," he said, referring to Mrs. Copeland's denial of knowing the men when officers first came to her house nearly a year earlier.

"She lied," he repeated.

Prosecutors felt the list recovered from the Copeland kitchen was a key in the murder case against her.

"What's the significance of that 'X'," Doug Roberts asked the jurors. "I guess we'll have to figure that out, won't we?"

Attorney Roberts was picking up a head of verbal steam by this point, and zeroing in on a rundown of each victim and how much money the Copelands made from their deaths. During his description of Dennis Murphy, he digressed briefly.

"We've heard that Faye Copeland collected old clothes to make rags or even quilts . . . to make a quilt of a dead person's clothes is enough to make a person vomit."

The sarcasm spilled over in his rundown of the year 1986, the first year officers had proof of the Copelands' involvement in the bad check and killing scheme: "1986 was a very good year for Faye and Ray."

Roberts's anger toward the now weeping Faye Copeland continued, as he noted that if they could have purchased a major carload of cattle with Jack McCormick, maybe they would have made enough money "to take a vacation from killing."

He further honed his attack on Mrs. Copeland.

"Faye Copeland was actively involved in this scheme. She cooked for them, she did their laundry, she was a Mom to them and, in a more sinister role, she was the security guard and she was the bookkeeper.

"Paul Jason Cowart was buried in his shirt and underwear, and was probably shot in bed.

"If she didn't participate, she knew about it.

"He was shot in the bedroom next to her. How could she not know?"

Roberts returned to the list, using a chart that was a photographic blowup of the scrap of paper.

"Dead men don't talk, but they scream . . .

"Freeman . . .

"Cowart . . .

"Harvey . . .

"All are on that list.

"I think 'X' means they're dead. 'X' marks the spot. 'X' is to cross out, on a typewriter.

" 'X' means they're dead."

The jury listened intently.

"That woman," he said, again angrily

pointing toward Faye, "acted with her husband to kill five men. She knew everything, she wasn't passive."

Perhaps anticipating Miller's "overbearing husband" defense, Doug Roberts continued.

"There's no way for her not to have known what was going on. I have what I consider to be a traditional marriage . . . and my wife knows what I'm thinking, she can almost finish a sentence for me."

If Faye Copeland was a victim, as David Miller had said in his opening remarks, Roberts wanted to know: "Who dumped her down a well? Who buried her in three inches of dirt? She was a victim, alright, a victim of her own stupidity and greed."

The jury seemed a little winded by the frankness and brutality of the closing remarks, compared to the legal tap-dance that often softens sharp issues during the other parts of a trial like this one.

They waited for David Miller's rebuttal.

"This case is not versus Mr. and Mrs., not versus Ray and not versus Ray and Faye," Miller said to the jurors. "Certainly, Ray Copeland plays a part, but the ultimate question is whether Faye 'aided or worked together' with her husband. You will have to find that she did something."

Miller had hoped that Jack McCormick's testimony could be splintered during his earlier cross-examination of the drifter, but that really didn't happen.

But, he still hammered at the credibility, or lack thereof, of the colorful McCormick.

"Jack McCormick is not a latter day Lone Ranger here . . . the message is only as good as the messenger," he said.

"No one saw her (Faye) shoot anybody, we all agree to that," Miller said. "Did she aid and abet? The evidence is circumstantial. Jack McCormick's skull and bones notwithstanding, nothing was found on the Copeland farm.

"Much of the evidence presented here has no importance to this lady over here. There was no blood on a mattress, no bullet hole.

"Ray's the one who hired people, there's nothing to link her to the sale barns, bank accounts, the hiring of the drifters.

"And, as to the clothing in the closet, the closet (was) crammed full of clothes for years. It wasn't out of the ordinary for clothing to be left behind.

"The letter? Just take it at face value.

"And now the list. Maybe she was trying to figure out what was going on on her farm. The list was prepared and Ray told her what happened. Maybe she hid it away from Ray . . . she was delving into Ray's business after all."

He then tried to lay out a little sympathy for the distraught Faye Copeland.

He cited her good work at the motel, and said the jurors needed to decide what kind of homelife Faye must have had.

"This is a woman who at least emotionally is abused, isolated, alone. When they argued, she was told to shut her mouth and that's when it ended. She didn't inquire about what Ray did. She knew there were some things you could talk about, others you can't. He dominated his wife, his children.

"Even if she tried to help him, he wouldn't let her. This is a lady who for years walked an emotional tightrope. She created an imaginary world for herself. If it wasn't the way Ray said it should be, she'd shut her mouth.

"I'm not asking for sympathy here, but (I) want you to think about what you're dealing with.

"Give her a chance to go out and rebuild a life for herself."

Doug Roberts and Kenny Hulshof had determined before the trial that they would split the double-sided prosecution closing remarks, with Roberts going for the anger and Hulshof going for the gut.

After a dramatic pause, his voice breaking slightly, Hulshof slowly, deliberately, held up 8 x 10 black and white photos of the five victims, and carefully pealed off their names.

He listed their survivors, slowly, dramatically.

"Each of them was lured here under the guise of a cattle operation but were murdered by Faye Copeland and her husband. Each was unsuspecting.

"They say Faye is a victim. A victim of what? A victim of who? Was her name on the list with an 'X'?

"But, in a way, she is a victim: a victim of the truth. She shall be shot down by the facts, buried in the evidence."

Attorney Hulshof seemed to counter effectively the defense efforts at portraying Faye Copeland as a victimized wife and mother.

"She grew up in the Depression, and came out as a survivor. They were married 50 years, for better, for worse . . . she's a strong-willed woman, an independent woman.

"Faye has tears," he continued, looking back toward her. "And don't doubt those tears, but ask why's she crying?

"Is it because her horrible crime has finally been exposed? Finally, maybe, she's realized the grief she and her husband caused. Maybe she's finally realized the gravity of what she and her husband accomplished."

The jury's instructions included the option of second degree murder, a lesser charge, and Kenny hammered at that plan.

"This is no second degree murder case, ladies and gentlemen of the jury. Every time Faye fixed breakfast, did laundry, anything to cultivate their trust, that makes her guilty."

As to Jack McCormick: "He was credible, believable . . . and he admitted to being a tramp, an alcoholic, and he's certainly a colorful character, but the harsh words from the defense about him just don't fly."

On to the list: "The 'Xs' were on a scorecard of death. She was right there in the thick of it all."

The letter: "There's one piece of evidence that should eliminate all doubts . . . the letter. I want you to get that letter and read it and talk about it. It was written four days after their arrest.

"She wrote, 'Things will cool down.' Well, I'm sorry, Mrs. Copeland, it hasn't cooled down, it's heated up.

"We've exposed you and your husband and your vile, horrible crimes."

The jury adjourned about 1:00 P.M. on a

quiet Saturday. Cars and trucks circled the courthouse at midday, and a few Christmas decorations were starting to show up in store windows.

At 4:05 P.M. that Saturday afternoon, the courtroom and its staff suddenly sprang back to life. The jury had been out barely three hours, and had signaled they had a verdict.

Faye Copeland was led back in the courtroom, and buried her face in her hands as she sat down.

The jury foreman quickly read the verdict: Guilty of murder in the first degree.

Faye Copeland mouthed, "I never done nothing."

The first phase of the trial was over: The jury would come back Monday and now decide whether she should be in prison for life without parole, or if she should be executed with a lethal injection.

Missouri's first degree murder statutes call for separate trials: The first for guilt or innocence, and then a second trial, right on the heels of the initial hearing, to determine the penalty. If the jury is unable to decide the penalty, the judge can set the sentence, or the judge can, but seldom does, overrule the life or death decision made by jurors.

As a part of the second phase, David Miller introduced testimony from one of the couple's sons and their only daughter, attempting to paint a picture of a woman dominated by an overbearing, cruel, cold husband.

Bonnie Copeland, Wayne's wife who is a correctional officer at a prison not far from Chillicothe, said it was her opinion that Ray Copeland treated his wife "like trash." She said "Ray made the decisions, she followed."

Betty Copeland Gibson, who now lives in Kentucky, painfully recounted growing up in the Copeland house, noting that she had "moved out" when she was eighteen. "My dad ran the home, his word was final and we knew when the word came down to shut up.

"My mom idolized my dad, but she knew her place and she knew when to shut up," the daughter said, her agony obvious.

"I never heard him tell her he loved her," she said, her head bowed.

Al Copeland, who also left home well before his twentieth birthday, said, "My father tried to domineer her.

"You did it his way or no way," Al said. "I think he treated her a lot worse than trash."

241

Marilyn Hutchison, a Kansas City psychologist, took up most of the defense portion of the second phase of the trial, with a long analysis of how she saw Faye Copeland.

"She was controlled by him for decades," she said.

She said some of her examination of Faye had revealed what she termed a "learned helplessness," where the woman "learns it doesn't work to stand up to someone" like Ray Copeland.

However, another medical expert, this time from the prosecution stable, said he found Mrs. Copeland to be "vigorous and a hard worker."

Dr. Richard Jacks, from the state hospital in nearby St. Joseph, said he saw "pride, she held her head up high, said she'd been working nonstop since the Great Depression, and was anticipating retirement."

He said, in response to questions, that he didn't find her to be dominated or to have any sort of personality disorder.

Faye Copeland never took the stand, in either phase of the trial, and many observers viewed that as perhaps a tactical error. It's not clear whether she wanted to testify, although she now claims she wanted to in at least the penalty phase of the trial. But she may have heeded David Miller's advice to not take the stand, although he could not have kept her from testifying if she had really wanted to. Defense lawyers often fear having clients take the stand, afraid whole new areas of testimony may be opened, and the client may be damaged. However, as one member of the prosecution team said later, "At least she could have gone up there in the penalty and looked at the jury and said 'Don't kill me.' That would have been effective."

Then it was time for closing arguments, and Attorney Hulshof once again went to the emotional level with the jury.

"You're going to have to dig down for just a little more courage," Kenny Hulshof said.

Then he went for a bit of a stretch: Referring to the "LA street gangs," and their raging violence in the urban areas, the young prosecutor said, "When I thought about this case and Ray and Faye Copeland and I began to weep . . . right here in our own backyards the same things, innocent victims being slain for profit."

Hulshof then backed away from the LA street gangs and got the case back to Livingston County.

"This case is really about greed, the hunger for money," he said, picking up the stack of photos of the victims he'd used in the closing arguments of the first phase of the trial.

"These individuals meant no more to these people than. . . ." and he wadded up the pictures and slammed them to the floor, chanting a word with each tossed picture:

"Lured . . .

"Deceived . . .

"Recruited . . .

"Betrayed . . .

"Murdered.

"Their lifeless bodies were scattered around this county like so many wads of paper."

Then he turned toward the weeping Faye Copeland.

"If there's anyone in this courtroom who believes in the death penalty, it's that woman," he said, pointing at Mrs. Faye Copeland.

"These young men were not from well-to-do families, and perhaps were not men you'd invite to your home," he continued. "But they had a right to live.

"There's never been a more complete and utter disregard of the sanctity of life than in this case of Faye Copeland.

"Stand firm."

David Miller, who had a couple of days to get over the disappointment and surprise of the quick conviction of his client, reminded the jurors again who was on trial.

"Recall who it is that we're talking about here," he said quietly, slowly. "We heard more about Ray Copeland than Faye Copeland . . . at whose doorstep are we going to place the blame here?

"She tried to protect her children from a man who wasn't a very good father . . . but did she pull the trigger? Did she do the things that caused these deaths?

"Ray Copeland ran his wife's life.

"You've said Faye Copeland participated in (this crime) but I do say to you Faye Copeland was not the dominant party in this scheme, she was the follower.

"She was totally dominated by her husband . . . I can't put that out as an excuse, but you can consider it."

Miller then tried to move what he saw as lifesaving arguments to a more emotional level.

"I've got a couple of kids, and I have to discipline them every now and then, to make a decision, then I have second thoughts. I usually start thinking I was too harsh, and rarely think I was not harsh enough.

"The decisions here today, well, if you're too harsh, it's final . . . there's no turning back.

"I hope for your sake you don't put yourself in a position to look back once in a while and wonder.

"You'll regret the death penalty. I ask you to say No to death."

Doug Roberts took a deep breath and moved toward the jury, the second part of the long trial nearing an end. He'd never asked a jury to take a life.

"This is a very sad and sordid affair," he said quietly. "And a humbling one . . . you have an awesome and terrible responsibility."

He shifted quickly to the medical experts who'd examined Faye Copeland.

He branded Dr. Hutchison as a "psychological Will Rogers—she never met a woman who she didn't think was battered."

He then asked the jury to remember three numbers and the reasons for them:

Five: "The victims, their bodies growing cold."

$32,000: "That's what they were killed for. That's about $1,000 a month, folks, an annuity, a retirement fund."

And, *69:* "The age of Faye Copeland when

246

they were killed. Age was no obstacle in killing, no hurdle for her. It didn't stop her, and it shouldn't stop you."

In one of his only references to David Miller, Roberts said, "He asked you to say No to death. But what about every man who walked into her house . . . it was heads you live, tails you die and are buried or dumped down a well.

"I really don't know how you can say No to a woman who always said Yes."

Following the jury's exit to the deliberation room, a drained Doug Roberts peered out a courtroom window for several minutes, his hands braced against the windowsill as if he were frozen.

Again, in about three hours, the jury signaled its verdict.

The courtroom quickly filled, and Al Copeland moved to the defense table to sit with his mother.

The decision was death on four counts, life without parole on one count, the first victim who died before the check charges could be filed against him.

Faye Copeland was nearly hysterical, her hands across her face. Her son tried to comfort her, in vain.

"This is not a happy occasion," Doug Roberts said as he left the courtroom.

Outside the courtroom, a tradition for him, David Miller lit a cigar and sighed. "I really don't want the jurors to be haunted by what they've done. I don't want to lay that on anybody."

Jack McCormick had had enough of his boardinghouse room, and found some liquor.

Before the night was over, he'd gotten the itch to move on, and walked south from Chillicothe, taking those steps of a man who'd had too much to drink, like he was stepping up and over something with each pace.

He was arrested a couple of miles south of Chillicothe and slept it off in the jail before heading back to the Victory Mission in Springfield.

The morning after the verdict, with the execution sentence handed down, Sheriff Leland O'Dell was taking Ray Copeland to a Kansas City hospital for further mental examinations.

"You hear about the verdict, Ray?" the sheriff asked.

"Nah . . . what happened?"

"Well, they found her guilty and recommended execution for her, Ray," the sheriff said carefully.

"Well those things happen to some, y'know. . . ."

Ray Copeland never asked again.

Chapter Fifteen

Kenny Hulshof almost dreaded what the ringing telephone might mean.

The past two days had been frantic ones, and he knew something was about to blow up around him: Livingston County Prosecuting Attorney Doug Roberts was wanting to make a plea agreement deal to avoid taking Ray Copeland to trial.

For Hulshof it was unthinkable, an option that shouldn't be on the table at this point. A jury had quickly, neatly convicted Faye Copeland and sentenced her to death, and the case against Ray Copeland was much better, a much more convincing set of facts. The case was a lead pipe cinch, and he knew it.

The budding friendship between Hulshof and Roberts was strained, at best, by the startling developments, and it was going to get nothing but worse.

County prosecutors and "loaned" attorneys from the state's Attorney General's office walk a thin diplomatic line, anyway, and Kenny had tried to rein in his eagerness and defer to Doug Roberts. But Roberts, sticking to his lower keyed style, had allowed Kenny Hulshof to take a bigger and bigger piece of the political, legal, and publicity pie. The reporters and camera personalities were naturally drawn to the outgoing Hulshof; while Roberts could have courted the favor of the media, he usually chose not to, but was displeased with the attention his fellow lawyer got.

In Chillicothe, an aggressive Barbara Schenkenberg and Pat Berrigan, the public defenders for Ray Copeland, were talking hard and fast with Doug Roberts, hoping to keep their elderly client off death row. The case against Ray Copeland was such that the public defenders would relish a sentence of life in prison without the chance of parole, and almost regard that as "winning." Doug Roberts, despite the success of the Faye Copeland trial, was getting tired and skittish about a second trial: What if something went wrong, and the jury freed Ray Copeland? What if the growing cost of the trials became an issue in his home political base of Livingston County? What if Ray Copeland died, and they were left with Faye Copeland sentenced to be executed?

Doug Roberts was getting ready to strike a deal, a situation he saw as a "win" for him and the county and yet still extreme punishment for the Copelands.

Roberts would settle for a guilty plea from Ray Copeland, and a sentence of life in prison without parole, and agree that Faye Copeland's sentence also be reduced to life without parole. The case would be over, clean and simple, and the Copelands would die in prison.

All the scurrying around, the deals between the local prosecutor and team of public defenders working for Ray Copeland came just hours before jury selection was supposed to get under way in Rolla, Missouri, nearly three hundred miles away from Chillicothe.

But, on the eve of kicking off a sure-thing case, with the prosecution having virtually all the cards, Hulshof could see no reason to back up now and take a plea bargain that would put both Copelands in prison, without parole, until they died. Ray Copeland's only requirement would be to plead guilty. Kenny Hulshof wanted more.

Judge Richard Webber and the staff of courtroom assistants were ready for the jury selection work to begin; Kenny Hulshof was ready.

But now Roberts was about to approve a plea bargain, much to the irritation of Hulshof and his bosses in the Attorney General's office in Jefferson City.

In Rolla, the proceedings were to get under way in a bizarre setting: A onetime store building on Pine Street that had been converted into a courtroom of sorts. Plate glass windows fronted the small city's main street, and folding chairs were lined up for reporters and observers.

The weeks since Faye Copeland's trial had been odd enough, with a flurry of motions and counter-motions from defense lawyers about Doug Roberts's onetime representation of the Copelands in the civil matters three years before they were both charged with first degree murder.

Chief Public Defender Pat Berrigan, who aimed to take a much more aggressive role in defense of Ray Copeland than David Miller had taken in defense of Faye Copeland, had filed a motion seeking to disqualify Roberts.

A week before the Rolla proceedings were to begin, Judge Richard Webber had overruled that motion, in a four-page decision, saying that no conflict of interest existed and Doug Roberts could prosecute the case.

But Judge Webber also was opposed to the growing talk of a plea bargain and found himself in an uncomfortable position.

The telephone lines between Jefferson City (Kenny Hulshof) and Chillicothe (Doug Roberts) and Kansas City (the public defenders) and Memphis, Missouri (Judge Webber) were buzzing the weekend before the January 24, 1991 kickoff date for the Ray Copeland jury selection.

Doug Roberts had been told by Kenny Hulshof after the Faye Copeland decision that a plea bargain was his option. "It's your county, you'll have to live with it," the state prosecutor told Roberts. But Hulshof also made it clear he didn't like the idea one little bit.

Doug Roberts wrestled with the idea for several days, knowing that a Ray Copeland conviction and sentence of death was very likely, but also knowing that getting guilty pleas from both Faye and Ray Copeland and getting a life-with-no-parole sentence wasn't too bad a deal either. And then it would be over.

There had been growing concern about the

mounting costs for Livingston County, though the county's reserves meant the government wouldn't go broke, only be out a lot of cash. Also, some local Livingston County residents were getting tired of the continuing negative press coverage and the way the trials were starting to dominate everyone's life in the area. And, the age of the pair made it very likely they would cheat the executioner by dying before the state could kill them.

Doug Roberts finally decided he'd take the offer.

The final details were pretty well nailed down by January 18 or so, even though Judge Webber still voiced misgivings in the patched-together telephone calls.

Hulshof was also starting to buck up, finally telling Roberts that if the plea bargain was sought, the Attorney General's office would pull out of the case.

Roberts had also decided that if the case came to trial, despite Judge Webber's ruling that no conflict of interest existed, he might have to withdraw to protect the case on further appeals.

The angles, the prospects, were swirling.

Tuesday afternoon before the scheduled Thursday start-up, a telephone conference call was set up between all sides, and all parties reluctantly agreed to the plea bargain, with Judge Webber unhappy, but apparently resigned to the action to come.

Following the conference call, Kenny Hulshof indicated to the judge he planned to withdraw and said he would not attend the Thursday hearing in Rolla.

Judge Webber later indicated Hulshof should come anyway.

That Thursday in Rolla, it appeared all the agreements were made, and Roberts showed up thinking he would be ready to start in the jury selection efforts.

What quickly transpired that Thursday morning was later described by Doug Roberts as "the strangest thing I ever saw."

The legal motions announcing the deal were briefly outlined in the packed small courtroom, and then Judge Webber dropped the bomb shell.

He said he was removing Roberts from the case, changing his mind about the earlier decision about potential conflict of interest, and was appointing Kenny Hulshof to prosecute the case.

The stunned lawyers momentarily froze.

Public defender Pat Berrigan appeared to be roaring mad: Doug Roberts was stunned and gathered up his papers and prepared to leave; Kenny Hulshof was perhaps just as stunned, thinking he was only a few minutes away from being removed from the case, but instead finding that it was his.

Berrigan, more or less able to confine his anger, addressed Judge Webber, questioning "whether the court has a predisposition in this case."

The highly unusual attack on a judge continued: "The intent of this court's ruling is clear: To subvert the prosecutor's desire to waive the death penalty."

Those were indeed strong words, heard as Doug Roberts is moving to a chair off to the side of the room, his face still reflecting the stunning developments of the past few minutes.

Hulshof then added to the startling developments, saying he'd rather go to jail than take over the case. His rash statement was based on the assumption that if he took the case, he'd have to honor the plea agreement, an assumption that proved to be wrong.

The proceedings were finally gaveled to a halt, and the crowd began to disperse. Judge Webber took the highly unusual step of having an impromptu press conference at the door to the courtroom, saying "Plea bargaining is inappropriate in some cases."

Doug Roberts, who'd driven to Rolla that morning with Chillicothe *Constitution-Tribune* reporter Ed Crawford, refused comment,

258

and finally turned to Crawford, saying, "Let's go home." They quietly left.

The Rolla blowup finally brought the long-whispered rumors of "politics" to the surface.

The rumors—the gallery whispers—had it that Judge Webber wanted to be promoted within the state's judicial ranks, say to a state appeals court or the like; that Kenny Hulshof was young and ambitious and might even like to seek elective office someday; and that Attorney General Bill Webster certainly wanted to be at least governor, riding the image of a "hangin' prosecutor" to higher office.

All the parties, naturally, denied those reports.

"If we don't seek the death penalty in a case as brutal as this one, if we don't aggressively prosecute people charged with killing five persons, when do we?" Hulshof said. "There's no politics in a case like this."

Roberts said later that several factors went into his deciding for a plea bargain that would have imprisoned both Copelands until they died.

"We had a trial for Faye Copeland and there was a therapeutic effect to it locally. I felt it was time to put this behind us. If we take today with the appeals process, Ray Copeland would be executed on March 7, 2002. Age doesn't bother me. Age alone is not important, or even a decided factor. But if you put that together with a mental condition, can you justify spending the money to execute him in a state that can't properly fund education? We are spending money to see that a seventy-six-year-old man gets what he deserves rather than spending it to give a sixteen-year-old what he deserves. The factors of Ray Copeland's age, the duration of the appellate process which is ten to twelve years, and the Mooresville man's deteriorating mental condition all played a role in this decision. Those factors made executing him remote, at best, if he got the death penalty. I will admit, however, that I've never had a tougher decision to make in my professional career."

But a few weeks after the disqualification of a county prosecutor—a highly unusual move—Roberts had this to add. "I'm disappointed in the manner in which I was treated by people I thought were my friends. There's more ambition here than I can understand. I just want to pay my mortgage, I don't want to be governor. I did what I thought was right, and even if it was wrong, it was still my decision. The Attorney General doesn't elect the Prosecuting Attorney, and a circuit judge doesn't elect the Prosecuting Attorney. That's about all I'm going to say."

It wasn't all that was going to be said, but now Kenny Hulshof had to take a cram course in Ray Copeland and get ready to single-handedly take the case to a jury. Because of the blowup in Rolla, the jury selection there proved impossible and after several days the process was moved to St. Louis County.

The jurors were picked on March 6 and the trial for the crusty old farmer began on March 7, 1991.

Chapter Sixteen

In the several months since Ray Copeland had first been arrested, his scowling, sometimes snarling, face had become a familiar one on the evening news and in the morning newspapers.

When he was first photographed, he was wearing his customary dark blue bib overalls, his massive, gnarled hands cuffed in front. He would look past photographers and gawkers, and be zipped in and out of the courthouse or jail quickly and quietly.

Later, after he and his wife appeared together for pretrial hearings, he was wearing garish, bright orange jail-issue coveralls. His expression had turned a little more serious, as if he were beginning to sense, a little perhaps, for the first time, the deep trouble he was probably in.

When trial time rolled around in Chillicothe, on Thursday, March 7, 1991, Ray Copeland was out of the overalls and the orange jumpsuit, but was still handcuffed and heavily guarded.

Now he was wearing a new open-collared pale blue dress shirt and gray slacks, and occasionally a light jacket against the early morning cool. He was cleaned up, wearing a hearing aid almost every day, and he kept his eyeglasses in a black case stuck in his shirt pocket. The "grandfather" look was complete.

Sheriff Leland O'Dell and other deputies saw to it that the courthouse lobby and stair landings were devoid of spectators clear up to the third-floor courtroom, and quickly took Ray Copeland to his day in court.

Doug Roberts was a floor below the courtroom, in the small prosecuting attorney's office. He had to briefly discuss the failed plea bargain in open court before the Ray Copeland proceedings could begin, in a "for the record" move by the court and Roberts. But before the trial began, Roberts was back downstairs, rudely rejecting an offer by Kenny Hulshof to allow him to stay in the courtroom despite his status as a witness.

Kenny Hulshof had tried to be civil with Doug Roberts, but the efforts weren't really taking.

Doug Roberts was back down in his office,

tending to the normal duties of the day, but was kept informed of each day's activities by others in the courtroom, including reporters he trusted.

He was never back in the Livingston County courtroom during the entire Ray Copeland trial.

Kenny Hulshof knew the courtroom, and the players, and, of course, the details of the Copeland case very well by now. But he also knew that the three-person public defender team huddled around Ray Copeland would mean a stouter defense effort than perhaps developed during the Faye Copeland proceedings. He knew that he was doing this case without the local prosecutor's help, and he knew that anything less than a full conviction and execution verdict for Ray Copeland would fly in the face of the strong verdicts against Faye Copeland.

While he felt sure the case against the crusty old farmer was a rock-solid one, he also knew that mistakes here, mistakes that could mean a lesser sentence against Ray Copeland, would be disastrous. How could you end up with a guilty verdict, and an execution order, against Faye Copeland and a lesser penalty against the person they all agreed was the ringleader of the sordid operation?

And, this was a different jury, a more urban mix of six men and six women, individuals who hadn't heard much about the case and might not be as shocked by the violence and the gory photos as the previous rural jury that heard the case against Faye Copeland.

Kenny Hulshof, nervously restacking the papers in front of him, breathed deeply, pushed himself up out of his chair and carefully walked over to the jury box to face the final arbiters of the complex case.

". . . This trial is like a book — a best-selling novel," Hulshof said.

"But this is not a book you can turn to the last page, however. It is a biography of a man who, over the course of three years, executed five men," he said, quietly but firmly and steadily.

He then outlined the scheme he and so many in the courtroom had become familiar with: recruiting the workers, setting up the checking accounts and post office boxes, passing the bad checks, and, finally, the killings. He listed the victims, slowly, deliberately.

"You're going to have to read this book page by page," he said. "There are many pieces of evidence to (be) presented. Please be patient as we prove this case."

Proof of Kenny Hulshof's concerns about the different defense lawyer team surfaced during the opening statement, with ten objections and hushed conferences at the judge's bench. Traditionally, a little more latitude is allowed by opposing lawyers in opening and closing remarks, but not this time.

Defense lawyer Martin Warhurst opened for the Ray Copeland team, rejecting the "best-selling book" analogy Hulshof had just used.

"This is more like a jigsaw puzzle, or like one from a garage sale, where there are three puzzles in one box, and they won't go together and make a picture," Warhurst said.

The defense lawyers also attempted to lay the groundwork for a big part of their defense: Ray Copeland was senile, and had serious physical and mental health problems. Warhurst said they would prove that the old farmer suffered from "progressive brain damage."

Warhurst also tried to chip away at the credibility—or lack thereof—of the yet-to-appear witness Jack McCormick, noting that despite the transient's story to the Nebraska hot line, there was never a trace of any body or body parts found on the Copeland farm.

Then, when it came McCormick's turn to

take the witness stand, he was instantly at odds with the defense lawyers, finally objecting at their attempts to describe his string of bad checks and the subsequent deal he made to drop charges in turn for his testimony. "This has no bearing here, no bearing on this case, except to make me look bad," he snapped. "I do not deny, and never have denied, that I've been bad."

Some of the initial drama of the Faye Copeland trial was lost in the Ray Copeland proceedings, because it was basically a repeat of the same case. There was little new evidence to hear.

So it seemed that, despite the intentness of the jurors and the lawyers for both sides, the trial of Ray had a somewhat lighter side. The tension was nowhere as great, inside or outside the courtroom.

When Harry Wolfe testified about Jack McCormick's taking the old clunker of a Pinto and not coming back, there were snickers at some of his references to McCormick. He identified a photo of McCormick with a smirk, "Yep, that's my friend Jackie." At one other point in his testimony, Wolfe shot up out of his chair, grabbing the back of his leg and fairly well shouting, "I got a cramp . . . can I stand up?"

Judge E. Richard Webber was able to keep the trial from getting completely informal, but it was more of an effort than during the previous hearings.

The spectators were becoming increasingly sophisticated about the proceedings, knowing early on that the key days (for them anyway) were going to be the closing arguments and during the second, or penalty, phase of the trial. There was little doubt that the old farmer was going to be found guilty, and quickly.

The closing arguments came after a weekend of preparation for Hulshof, who'd grown more confident each day of the trial.

He felt sure that the jury was ready to convict Ray—knowing all the while that thinking you are ready a jury correctly is a high risk game.

He opened his closing remarks with the photos of the victims, similar to the approach in the closing arguments in the Faye Copeland proceedings.

"These men all had two things in common," he said.

"First, each was a drifter, a free spirit who longed for respectability, who asked for a chance to escape the soup kitchens and the streets. They became easy marks for that man, Ray Copeland," he said, turning to point his finger at Copeland, who occasionally fidgeted with his hearing aid and seemed to listen to most of the testimony each day.

"Secondly, they made a fatal mistake, each met and trusted the defendant, not aware of his hunger and his lust for money.

". . . This defendant is a shrewd man, he knows cattle are difficult to trace, (he knows) how long the bank takes to clear a check, and so forth.

"He even asked that the men not bring cars if they had them . . . he knows bodies are easier to dispose of than vehicles."

The final step, Hulshof told jurors, was to "execute the men . . . you can't have witnesses hanging around. Dead men tell no tales.

"These men died, their only payment for their work was pieces of metal in the head."

Defense lawyer Pat Berrigan, who was still angry at the developments from Rolla weeks before and what he saw as one-sided justice in the days of the trial, kept his cool in the closing arguments.

He reminded jurors that a "man's liberty and a man's life is at stake here," and said they must make their decision "beyond any reasonable doubt."

"There is zero direct evidence that Ray Copeland killed anyone," Berrigan said. "No one saw him ... it's only circumstantial: Bodies, a gun, a list of names, Jack McCormick. . . ."

He then broke down the findings for the jury.

"The bodies, three were found on the Bryant farm—that barn's not Ray Copeland's, and it's miles from his home; the well on the Adams's property is miles from Ray Copeland's home. If Ray Copeland wanted to bury bodies, why not put them on his own farm?

"The gun—Who owns the gun? Are there any fingerprints? Any testimony here that it's his gun? We have to take their word for it.

"The list—is Ray Copeland's name anywhere on that list? He's on trial here, and you're being asked to speculate."

He then aimed his fire at Jack McCormick, just as the defense lawyers for Faye Copeland had attempted, without success, a few months earlier.

"He's a proven liar ... his testimony is not subject to belief.

"Jack McCormick just out and out lied about the bodies on the Copeland farm."

Pat Berrigan's next tactic was to remind jurors, if they needed reminding, of the seriousness of their pending decision.

"You have to live with this decision the rest of your life," he said, looking directly at the jurors.

Then, as he had been doing often during the trial, Pat Berrigan looked into the jurors' eyes, trying to get a reading as to their thoughts.

He apparently didn't like what he saw.

Turning away from the jurors and walking back to the defense table, Berrigan said, "We don't need to spend another week on this . . . God bless you."

He sat down, a glum look on his face. He knew he'd lost that jury, and that Ray Copeland was as good as convicted.

Kenny Hulshof, who had developed a solid relationship with opponent David Miller in the earlier Faye Copeland trial, had been angry at many of the tactics (he saw them as stalling and aggravating tactics) used during the Ray Copeland trial. He vented some of that anger, while politely, in the closing remarks.

"I wish I could answer every question for you, I wish there had been a video camera around," he said sarcastically. "But there wasn't."

He then defended his key witness: "Jack Mc-Cormick is not what this case is about. But, if Jack McCormick hadn't made that phone call, if Ray Copeland had succeeded in killing Jack McCormick, we would have never known about any of this."

Referring to notes he'd made during Berrigan's remarks, Hulshof answered the defense lawyer's points.

"Why didn't Ray Copeland bury the bodies on his property . . . He's a little smarter than that, he knew not to bury those bodies there."

But Hulshof saved his biggest verbal fireworks for his theme that Ray Copeland was continuing to thumb his nose at the law, as he had for years.

"Don't let him have the last laugh this time. "Stand firm."

In slightly more than two hours, the jury was back, walking steadily and with serious purpose back to their chairs. Most avoided eye contact with Ray Copeland.

The verdict was no surprise: guilty on all five counts of first degree murder.

Ray Copeland could be seen mouthing, "I'm OK," as his lawyers and the deputies led him back out of the courtroom.

Barbara Schenkenberg, one of the three defense lawyers representing Ray Copeland, had seemed emotionally drained watching the old farmer listen to the trial, sometimes his eyes indicating he understood very little.

But, she'd also known—or at least felt very certain—that the jury was going to convict Ray Copeland.

Her job was to try to save his life, what was left of it. During trial breaks, she'd enjoyed hearing of a flamboyant St. Louis public defender who had assailed a jury and almost shamed them out of sentencing a murderer to death. In the penalty phase of that trial, the St. Louis lawyer had told jurors, "Jesus died for scum-bags like" his client, and warned them that someday, "late some night," they would be haunted by sentencing a man to death. That jury backed up and told the judge to make the sentencing decision.

Schenkenberg didn't go that far, or with that flair, but she came close.

"You're entering a very awesome few days here," she told jurors.

"Ray Copeland is dying, there has been evidence of mental disease and defect. This is not offered as an excuse, but his brain is shriveling in his head as we sit here. He may not know why he's here.

"God is punishing Ray Copeland in a way, so you won't have to."

Dr. James Merikangas testified in the penalty phase of the trial, noting that he had found that Ray Copeland suffered from diabetes, high blood pressure, that he was deaf in his right ear, and had very low vision in his right eye: "clear evidence of (brain) shrinkage, as a result of strokes."

The doctor carefully termed Ray Copeland's problems as "much more than the normal aging process," and described elaborate schemes he said Ray Copeland had told him about, some of them deals involving mysterious cattle purchases and the like.

"He described an international cattle buying and selling conspiracy, and said you're in grave harm if you uncover it. He said, 'Just go into any cattle barn and be quiet and you'll hear all about it,' " the doctor said.

The testimony didn't seem to shake the jury, or at least their faces indicated no sympathy, no lenience, for Ray Copeland.

Kenny Hulshof walked close to the jury box and looked at the dozen persons squarely. "It took a lot of guts for you to convict Ray Copeland," he said quietly.

"It's not fair, but you're going to have to dig in and find that courage you found two days ago, that same courage to sentence Mr. Copeland to die from a lethal injection.

"It's tempting to take the easy path."

But the young prosecutor continued, after a brief pause, laying the tough decision squarely with the jury.

"You had the defendant pegged just right . . . you hit it right on the mark. The man has mocked our system for forty years.

"When is he going to take responsibility for his actions?

"Today."

He then zeroed in his attack on Ray Copeland.

"The grim reality of this case is that we have a hired killer in our midst," he said, again turning and pointing to Copeland. "He might wear a pair of work boots and bib overalls, but he has a wallet where his heart should be and he's a killer for cash."

The arrogance, the thumbing-his-nose-at-the-system theme appeared to be playing well to the jury; none seemed to flinch at the thought of sentencing the old farmer to die.

"Ray Copeland has thumbed his nose at the judicial system. When are we going to make him take responsibility?

"Today.

"If he," he said, turning again to point to Copeland, "had decided to make the right choice, he would have spared us all this agony."

* * *

Barbara Schenkenberg, clutching a notebook with her planned remarks, walked slowly to face the jury. "Ray Copeland is going to die in prison, that's no longer an issue.

"You will decide when.

"It is not necessary to execute Ray Copeland."

She then outlined what she saw as the three reasons to condemn someone to death.

"First, to condemn a heinous act; second, to punish Ray Copeland, who you have found guilty; and third, to protect society.

"You have already condemned his acts. In this society, we condemn senseless killing, and you've done that.

"You do not have to execute Ray Copeland to punish him . . . or to protect society.

"There are cases where (execution) may be necessary, but that is not the case here."

She then went to an emotional level with the stone-faced jury.

"Ray Copeland didn't show any mercy, but the truth is that we are not like that.

"We should be merciful and try to give life and not death . . . Ray Copeland didn't do that, but we can. He's going to die anyway. He's going to slip further and further.

"Ray Copeland is going to be no threat to

society when he is incarcerated . . . he'll be taken to prison where he will stay until he dies.

"The prosecutor might like for you to think somehow you're soft on crime if you don't impose the death penalty.

"But that is nonsense.

"To lock a seventy-five-year-old man into a cage . . . to say that is not punishment is nonsense.

"He will never see his wife of fifty years again. He may never see his children or grandchildren.

"He's socially dead now.

"It is not necessary for you to impose the death penalty."

As to his health, according to the defense attorney, "Can we say that Ray Copeland's brain damage didn't somehow affect him?

"He's responsible and you've held him responsible.

"But what if five years from now, three years from now, you start thinking 'Did I do the right thing?'

"If you regret this decision, there's no going back.

"We have a sacred love of life in this country.

"What if Ray tumbled over right now . . . people would rush up here to try to save his life . . . that's the way we look at it.

"I ask for mercy for Ray, pure and simple, unadulterated mercy . . . not because he gave it, because he didn't.

"But we can.

"It isn't necessary to kill Ray Copeland."

Drained, she slumped back in her chair at the defense table. Copeland's expression didn't change: He was simply looking at the jury as he had been oftentimes during the long and sometimes tedious trial.

Kenny Hulshof came back before the jury, his steps revealing an anger that he translated easily and quickly for the jurors.

"If there's one person in this courtroom who believes in the death penalty, it's him," he said loudly, turning and pointing again to Ray Copeland, who was fidgeting with his hearing aid and seemed once again to be listening intently.

"Age should not be a part of this case.

"The man knew right from wrong.

"Discussion closed."

Hulshof's voice was steadily rising.

"I'm not asking you to play God, but you are representatives of society, you mirror society.

"You can show Ray Copeland 'Here is what we think of you and your actions.'

"Innocent life is profoundly precious, whether you're a drifter, a transient, or whatever.

"Whose lives have less value, whose lives do we put more value on?

"This defendant has displayed an utter disregard for the sanctity of life."

Kenny Hulshof then reminded jurors of the book analogy he had opened the proceedings with.

"We have here the biography of a man, a serial killer, and the only thing to be done is to write the last page, which could be boiled down to three single words:

"Ray must pay!"

Judge Webber, munching on a Hardees sandwich and sipping iced tea at his bench, waited for the jury, which had left the courtroom about 7:00 P.M. No one roamed very far from the courtroom, feeling the jury would likely be back quickly.

They were right.

Not much longer than an hour later, they were back. The jurors seemed to have that same expression, one of agreement and firmness, that they had when they came back with the guilty verdict a few days earlier.

Ray should indeed pay, the jury said.

The unanimous decision: Death for Ray Copeland, by lethal injection.

In May after the March verdict, the parties in the case (minus, of course, Doug Roberts) all gathered again for the formal sentencing from Judge Webber, a decision that most assumed would be sure and simple. There seemed to be little doubt that the judge would follow the same pattern as he had with the Faye Copeland verdicts, and approve the execution order sending the couple to death row.

But the political mumblings and asides that had been bubbling around the Copeland cases for weeks and months finally surfaced, when defense lawyer Pat Berrigan rose and read an unprecedented and blistering attack on a whole series of people involved in the long trial. Judge Webber and Kenny Hulshof and others in the courtroom sat in stunned silence as Berrigan began. They really didn't know what to expect, but were startled when he started.

"The decision to kill Ray Copeland was made long before today. The Attorney General made it as part of a political decision when he flew to Chillicothe to announce to a press conference at Mr. Copeland's arraignment that the State would indeed seek the death penalty. It is sad enough that the Attorney General feels

281

that killing Ray Copeland will generate votes, because that may very well be true. Still, it makes one wonder to what depths politicians will sink to obtain public office.

"To some extent (Missouri Attorney General) William Webster's decision to seek the death penalty for political gain, although detestable, is still somewhat understandable. What is more repugnant and cannot be explained is this Court's decision to actively support that goal for whatever secret reasons harbored by the Court.

"There are few fundamental rights as important as the right to have an unbiased judge preside at one's trial and determine one's fate. It really matters little the skill of the defense attorneys, or the prosecutors, or the ability of the jury to decide the facts and apply the law accordingly, when the judge that presides over the trial has indicated a bias and prejudice against the defendant as was present in this case. The sham that took place on January 24, 1991, in the Phelps County courtroom in Rolla, Missouri is virtually unprecedented in the modern history of criminal jurisprudence in Missouri. For a judge to decide that the defendant's life will not be spared, and to substitute his judgment for that of the elected prosecutor in seeking the death of the defendant is unheard of. That the judge presided over the trial of the codefendant, and has evidenced not only satisfaction for that jury's verdict for death, but an active support for it, makes the refusal of the defendant's guilty plea in this case even more egregious.

"We have spent two hundred years refining the criminal justice process in this country. It is certainly not without its faults and its weaknesses, but it is the best system that we know of to ensure individual liberty while being able to effectively prosecute those who violate our laws. It is an adversarial system in which the prosecuting attorney, the defense counsel and the court have very distinct, separate and often conflicting roles. When one of the players fails to follow his role, then the system fails. When it is the judge that fails to abide by his oath, then the system not only fails, but it is brought dishonor, disgrace and a general distrust not only by those of us who work in it, but by the general public as a whole."

Berrigan had the floor, and there wasn't another sound in the courtroom. There were only a few people in the courtroom that day, most of them reporters seeking an end to the Copeland saga. Judge Webber's expression didn't change. He, as everyone else, was stunned.

Berrigan continued, reading from a prepared statement.

"This Court disqualified Douglas S. Roberts,

Jr., not because of any conflict with the defendant, but because the Court was dissatisfied with the proposed plea agreement that would spare Mr. Copeland's life. The agreement was particularly egregious to this Court because this Court had presided over a two-week trial of Mrs. Faye Copeland and was satisfied that the jury had come to the 'proper' decision, not only in its finding of guilt of first-degree murder 1, but in the recommended sentences of death by lethal injection. The Court made that evident during its conversations with defense counsel on Friday, January the 18 and Tuesday, January the 22. Then between January 22 and January 24 the Court surreptitiously contacted the Attorney General's office and advised them to be present in Rolla, Missouri after they had already clearly indicated they would not be taking part in the proceedings due to the guilty plea. Of course, the Court did not advise defense counsel that there would be no guilty plea and the actions of the Court on January the 24 came as a complete surprise.

"It is no wonder that defense counsel was surprised. Mr. Douglas S. Roberts, Jr., the elected prosecutor who had planned to proceed with the guilty plea, was shocked more than anybody. It has been the long-standing practice in Missouri that prosecuting attorneys, not judges, determine whether a plea agreement will be offered and what the substance of the agreement will be. Indeed, when judges take over this function, as was done here, they are no longer impartial arbiters but prosecutors themselves. It has been clear in this case, and that of Mrs. Faye Copeland, that this Court has never been other than an arm of the Attorney General's office.

"The instances during the trial of Mr. Ray Copeland at which the Court evidenced its predisposition toward the Attorney General's office are documented in the new trial motion filed by the defendant, and will be evident once the transcript is prepared of this trial. It ranges from the very first stages of the pretrial proceedings when the Court almost refused the defendant's request for mental evaluation because it did not want to postpone his trial, to its conduct during voir dire, particularly in Rolla, Missouri where it intentionally misrepresented defendant's position regarding the questioning of jurors on publicity in an effort to get the defendant to waive on the record his frequently stated position that individual publicity voir dire questions were necessary, to a slew of evidentiary rulings at trial too numerous to mention here, to permitting spectators to behave as though Court were a circus and their applause was to be expected and not condemned, to permitting state's witnesses to cry openly on the witness stand while jurors were also crying, while all the time refusing to grant the defendant's repeated requests for a recess, to submitting a capital murder case that had been in trial for four weeks at 7:00 P.M. at night under the ridiculous and unfounded reason that there was a flu epidemic in the city of Chillicothe, to taking a five minute recess during Mrs. Copeland's sentencing under the guise of deliberating about her fate when all the while the Court had already expressed its intention to carry out the recommendation of death that the jury had rendered."

Pat Berrigan took a deep breath, and continued. The court was still hushed, as he read on.

"The Court's obsession with having a thorough record belies the true function of an impartial judge, fairness and impartiality to the parties and the cause of action. Undoubtedly, when the transcript is reviewed by the appellate courts, as it assuredly will be, this Court will get high marks for its ability to cite case law and clean up the record for the prosecuting attorney when he was unable to intelligently respond to defense objections and arguments. If that is a measure of a judge, and I pray that it is not, then this Court will get high grades indeed.

"The role of a judge is not an easy one and only the best of our profession are hopefully considered for such a position. In my brief seven years in practice I have never had occasion to publicly criticize any judge for bias or prejudice toward my client. Although I may not have agreed with the judge's position, usually there was no question about their fairness or their impartiality. Here, that is not the case. As Mr. Copeland may perhaps spend his last years on death row, it is important that the public recognize that his guilt or innocence aside, he was entitled to the valuable protections affording us all under the Missouri and United States Constitutions. Mr. Copeland was denied those protections. When we cast aside these constitutional provisions in an effort to convict and punish the accused at any cost, then we become a nation not of laws but of men. That happened here."

Another deep breath for Berrigan, and he concluded, "I close by urging this Court, although I feel sure that my request is futile, to grant Mr. Copeland a new trial, to reinstate the elected prosecutor of Livingston County, Mr. Douglas S. Roberts, and to disqualify itself from further proceedings in this case.

"Thank you."

The silence held for a moment. Judge Webber was expressionless, Kenny Hulshof continued to fidget with his pencil and had a bit of an ironic smile on his face.

Swallowing deeply, and sitting upright, Judge Webber broke the silence by denying the request for a new trial.

The penalty for Ray Copeland: Death by lethal injection.

Dismissed.

Epilogue

The round-nosed shovels, well-worn and obviously very old, are held high by the auctioneer's ring man, clutching two of the tools in each hand.

The bidders elbow and crowd in around a long table cluttered with assorted hand tools, coils of rope and wire and other farm residue.

But the old shovels are moving the bidders to new heights. The bidding is aggressive, the interest is high.

"I hear seventeen? Eighteen? Hear nineteen dollars?" is the amplified chant from Lonnie Sewell on this crisp April Saturday morning. The repeated calls for bids echo out across the farm, the barns, out to a murky pond. Cars and dusty pickup trucks are jammed end-to-end along the narrow farm to market road leading to the small farm.

The auctioneer gets quick nods or slightly raised hands from the circling bidders, sending prices up.

The reason for the interest: The shovels are

Ray Copeland's.

They likely are the shovels the old killer used to dig the shallow graves of at least four of his victims.

And many people gathered here this Saturday seem eager to own one or a handful of the old tools.

They eventually draw winning bids of twenty-one dollars, not bad at all for well-used hand tools.

And maybe the eerie scene was a fitting close to the pain and anger and grief that had originated on this simple, peaceful-looking, little farm that had been home to Faye and Ray Copeland for more than two decades.

On April 6, 1991, sons Wayne and Al Copeland stood back out of the way, and let Lonnie Sewell and his auction company helpers move out the remnants of the Copelands' simple life. They seemed pained a little by the events, but also there was a sense of relief.

The Saturday farm auction has become a pattern in the fabric of life in Livingston County and through much of the farming areas. This sale, though, has drawn more than the usual bargain hunters and the bored and the nosy.

There were those here just for the bargains: twelve hundred dollars for an antique 1940s Massey Ferguson tractor, fifty cents for little wooden toys, eight hundred dollars for Faye

Copeland's 1978 Chevrolet station wagon, low-dollars for other hand tools and farm supplies.

But there were others here who viewed the auction as a way to end the Copeland saga, and, possibly, pick up a morbid souvenir of the horror that took place on the peaceful-looking acreage.

Some of those standing around want to know if Ray Copeland's old Marlin .22 caliber rifle, the one he used to execute at least five men, is going to be for sale. No, they learn. It is still held by the sheriff. No sale today.

"When you look around here, you can see that Mr. and Mrs. Copeland lived more humble lives than most of us," Lonnie Sewell said to the crowd as it formed up around the items to be sold. "Let's just forget about all the publicity about all this and just have fun."

Al Copeland says he's "glad to get it over," and sees the day's sale as a chance to clear a few more memories out of the way.

Wayne Copeland, who organized the sale, just watches and occasionally shakes his head at the low prices some items brought, items he thought might bring top dollar. Ray Copeland's 1984 pickup truck, the one he drove to homeless missions to pick up workers and the one he used to haul the bodies of his victims, brought a princely three thousand dollars. But items the boys had made in school or as craft projects when they were much younger brought pennies.

The sale grossed $9,250, with the auctioneer taking his cut and the seventy-five hundred net proceeds put into a special bank account that might someday go to the public defender's office to help defray the cost of the defense of the Copelands or to the county to help pay for the trial and jail time locally.

Not long after the auction, the Copeland children rented the old home place to Otis Harper and his family. "We needed a place to live, so we came here," Harper said. "It doesn't bother me what happened here. Why should it? I couldn't have done anything about it."

The Copelands were sent to separate prisons after their convictions, and there's a good chance they'll never see one another again.

Ray Copeland, only infrequently in touch with any of his family, invited reporters to "come and see me some time" after his conviction, but by early summer 1992 his diabetes had worsened and his general health was reportedly slipping.

Faye Copeland was placed in a women's prison in Jefferson City and appeared to have finally come to terms with her imprisonment and her life behind walls. There were even indications that she had found ways to productively fill her time, helping ill or crippled inmates, and that her health had rebounded. She was in frequent touch with her family, and the Chillicothe sons seldom if ever missed a chance to visit her.

Stacks of lengthy court appeals were filed, and will likely be heard over the next several months. Some court observers feel Faye Copeland's case may be overturned, perhaps because of a technical error in jury selection. Whatever, in cases where the death penalty is assessed, there is an automatic appeal process that takes the case to the state Supreme Court.

They are the oldest couple on death row in modern American history.

Like other states with the death penalty, the rituals and trappings of death are well established.

Inside the walls of the state's maximum security prison near Potosi, Missouri, contractors built a special room within a room. The windowed inner room contains a panel of electronic controls. The outer room contains two sets of risers that hold two rows of plastic chairs, aimed at the windows of the inner room.

It's the state's execution chamber, where condemned inmates breathe their last breath as the deadly chemicals race through their blood veins.

When court appeals finally run out on those on death row, they are sedated, intravenous tubes are placed in their arm, and they are strapped to a hospital gurney. Minutes before midnight they are wheeled into the small room and tubes from a machine about the size of a small refrigerator are connected to the tubes already in their arm.

The slatted blinds on the windows of the death chamber are still closed, and the warden quietly reads the death warrant to the condemned prisoner.

At a minute past midnight, the blinds are jerked open, and a special dispenser shoves the poison into the veins of the prisoner. Three prison officers, unknown to the general public, operate the machine, pushing their own buttons to send out the poison. They never know which button actually administers the lethal dosage.

The chemical hits the prisoner, who flinches slightly, his eyes open, then shut, and sometimes there's a slight shudder or jerking movement. Within seconds, they are dead and the blinds are re-closed.

Neat, clean, and . . . deadly.

That's what could await Faye and Ray Copeland, though the normal ten-year appeals process would seem to mean they could cheat the executioner.

The notoriety of the Copeland case drew reporters and television producers in the several weeks following the final verdict against Ray

Copeland.

Jack McCormick talked of writing a book, then dropped out of sight for a few weeks; Kenny Hulshof thought about the book notion, and then decided to stick to the law; Doug Roberts entered his notes into a home computer, hoping someday to tell his story; Ed Crawford of the Chillicothe paper talked himself out of a book project.

A production crew from "60 Minutes" found Chillicothe, and spent a couple of days highlighting what they saw as the pertinent elements of the case.

When the report, narrated by reporter Ed Bradley, finally aired in the winter of 1992, it featured bits and pieces of the saga of Jack McCormick, who willingly walked Ed Bradley through the Copeland barn and was filmed seriously filling his food tray at his home away from home, the Victory Mission in Springfield, Missouri.

McCormick repeated his story of Ray Copeland aiming his rifle at him while he was allegedly looking for a raccoon in the Copeland barn.

Ed Bradley and McCormick's use of the Copeland farm angered Wayne Copeland, who claimed the production crew trespassed on the family's property. He ordered the crew off the property, but only after they'd secured the footage they wanted.

"They had no right being here," Wayne Copeland said angrily. "They climbed over fences and broke into the barn."

That controversy passed.

And, certainly not by accident, Missouri Attorney General Bill Webster was the only lawyer associated with the report, the only attorney interviewed, even though he was never in the courtroom. He described the brutality of the crimes, and defended his office's aggressive pursuit of the death penalty. The public defenders, the county prosecutor, or even the state attorney handling the case, were never mentioned.

Following the airing of the report, public defender Pat Berrigan fired off an angry letter to the "60 Minutes" team.

"Unmentioned in your story was that Ray Copeland tried to plead guilty for the murders he committed, agreeing to be sentenced to life imprisonment without any chance of parole. His wife would have received the same sentence, saving the taxpayers at least two million dollars in trial expenses and legal fees for years of subsequent appeals. Bill Webster, running for governor, and Ray's trial judge, now up for the Missouri Supreme Court, would not permit the plea. The trial judge went so far as to disqualify the local prosecutor, who had agreed to the plea for life without parole, so that Webster's office could step in and seek death.

"Ray and Faye will die in prison even if they are not executed. Aside from the moral quagmire society enters, do we cherish the death penalty so dearly that we are willing to waste two million tax dollars to execute a seventy-six-year-old man and his seventy-year-old wife at the expense of our children's educations, and to enhance a somewhat sullied reputation as the only 'civilized' nation on earth where the government kills septuagenarians."

The letter was signed by Berrigan and fellow public defenders Martin Warhurst and Barbara Schenkenberg.

The Copeland sons, Wayne and Al, watched the telecast, and felt their mother was unfairly branded as guilty by the tone and pictures from the report. At one point Faye Copeland snapped at Ed Bradley, her cold eyes darting in his direction when he re-asked a question. It was not a look that won Faye any new supporters.

Amnesty International, from its world headquarters in London, entered the Copeland fray, in a letter to Bill Webster:

"I am writing regarding the case of Ray Copeland, who is awaiting sentencing in the Circuit Court of Missouri, Livingston County, after being convicted for a crime he committed when he was aged 71.

"Amnesty International is a worldwide, independent movement which works for the release of men and women, detained anywhere by reason of their beliefs, religion, sex, colour, language or ethnic origin provided that [they] have neither used nor advocated violence. Such prisoners are known to the organization as 'prisoners of conscience.' It also works for fair trials for political prisoners and opposed the death penalty, torture or other cruel, inhuman or degrading treatment or punishment of all prisoners.

"Amnesty International is concerned about the possible imposition of a sentence of death on Ray Copeland, noting that he was over the age of seventy at the time of the crime. This would contravene Article 4(5) of the American Convention on Human Rights which states:

"Capital punishment shall not be imposed upon persons who, at the time the crime was committed, were . . . over seventy years of age . . .'

"The U.S. government signed the American Convention on Human Rights in 1977 but has not yet ratified it. However, as a signatory nation the U.S. has an obligation under the Vienna Convention on the Law of Treaties to do nothing that would defeat the object of signed treaties. Amnesty International believes that all jurisdictions within the USA have a similar obligation to comply with recognized international standards.

"The organization is aware of the very serious nature of the crime for which Ray Copeland has been convicted. However, it requests that the above be considered when the case comes for sentencing and strongly urges that a sentence of death is not imposed on Ray Copeland. We would also request, on humanitarian grounds, that a sentence of death is not imposed on Mrs. Copeland, a co-defendant in the case.

"I am sending a copy of this letter to the Honourable Justice E. Richard Webber of Livingston County Circuit Court, who tried the case.

"(Signed) Ian Martin, Secretary General"

The plea fell on deaf ears.

In a jailhouse interview with *St. Joseph News-Press/Gazette* reporter Michael McCann, Faye Copeland sobbed that she simply wanted to go home.

"I want to go where I can be free, where I can work, get back my health and be myself. I just want to be myself again."

She was even beginning to waver in her seemingly endless loyalty to Ray when the interview was held.

"I'll always love him, but not as much now," she said. "He has done me great damage.

"I begged him time and time again to please

299

stay out of trouble. We had our home and everything paid for. We were on Social Security. So, why would he turn around and mess all that up just like he has?"

In the copyrighted interview, Faye continued to claim she had little or no knowledge of her husband's activities. "I was not involved in anything he did. I don't know where he picked them up or (where) they went," referring to the transients her husband hired as farmhands.

She says she was shocked to learn that the men found buried were the men hired to work on the family farm.

"I don't think there was anybody more surprised than me," she said. "He was always the father of my kids. I just loved him so much. It just doesn't seem right."

She also addressed the families of the dead workers.

"This life is too precious to take. God didn't put us here to take another life . . . I feel sorry for (the families). If there was any way I could bring them back, I would."

The Livingston County courthouse has returned to normal county business, and most here are happy about that.

The double murder trials cost the county more than two hundred thousand dollars, but reserve funds kept the treasury intact.

The key players in the months of investigation and trial have also continued with their lives.

Doug Roberts has been on the ballot since the failed plea bargain, and was handily re-elected. He continues as prosecuting attorney. He and Kenny Hulshof didn't exchange Christmas cards. At various prosecutors' meetings since the blowup between the two men, Hulshof has seemingly gone out of his way to speak to Roberts, and acts as if he wants the episode behind him.

Leland O'Dell and Gary Calvert are still sheriff and deputy, and still patrolling the county and dealing with the outlaws and politics of being the top law officers in the county.

David Miller is still based in the office across from the courthouse, still likes to light up a cigar at the end of a day in court, and still thinks the death sentence verdict for Faye Copeland "borders on the macabre."

Pat Berrigan continues as a public defender, though Barbara Schenkenberg has left the office.

Kenny Hulshof is still with the Attorney General's office, and is still trying high-profile murder cases. In a southwest Missouri murder trial of a woman charged with sawing up her mother and scattering parts of her alongside the road, Kenny Hulshof again used the "case reads like a novel" opening to the jury. His political future seemed in the summer of 1992 to center around reports that he might become the prosecuting attorney in one of the state's larger counties.

William Webster won the Republican nomination for governor in August. He lost in November.

Judge Richard Webber has four times appeared on the list of finalists for appointment to higher courts, but remains on the bench in Memphis, Missouri, a Democrat in a state run by Republicans.

Jack McCormick has fallen off the wagon a few times since the trials ended, but was featured in a segment of "60 Minutes" in the spring of 1992. He still can be found sometimes at the same Springfield mission where he was when Ray Copeland hired him.

While the families of the known victims have been able to finally grieve and bury their relatives, the agony of the Copeland terror continues for at least three more families.

Deputy Calvert, in his painstakingly meticulous system, has tracked at least three other men who had ties to Ray Copeland during the period when he was paying out his deadly wages.

*Thomas Park, fifty-two when he was last seen in February 1989, has not been located. Records indicate Ray Copeland hired the man February 17 of that year, and the drifter was last seen eleven days later. Park's sister attended the Ray Copeland trial, hoping that she'd be able to find information that could lead her to her brother, but none developed. "It's tearing me apart," said Park's sister Carolyn Barrett. "I know I'll never see him again."

*Franklin Hudson, forty-two when hired by Ray Copeland. The checks and address applications place Hudson with Ray Copeland from May 9 to May 20, 1989, according to Gary Calvert. His mother came to the Ray Copeland trial, hoping either Ray or Faye would "finally break down" and tell her something about her son. "I'd like to see Ray Copeland out in the desert on an anthill with syrup all over him," Ann Hudson said.

*Dale Brake, thirty-two when last seen, is linked to Ray Copeland from November 9 through November 11, 1988, according to Calvert's records. His sister came to the trials. Doris Hilliard said her missing brother was a father of four children. "There's no punishment enough for Ray Copeland," she said. "Or for her either, for that matter."

There's been no sign of the men or their bodies.

Authorities figure Ray Copeland made about thirty- to thirty-two thousand dollars with his cattle reselling scheme over a three year period.

They found eighteen one-hundred-dollar bills stashed in a small piece of pipe when they searched the farm.

That's all he had.